AN ESSENTIAL GUIDE TO PROPERTY MANAGEMENT

2 6 APR 2007

AN ESSENTIAL GUIDE TO PROPERTY MANAGEMENT

by

JOHN GREED, ROGER HEATH, MARK STEEL
AND SUE WOOD

2002

A division of Reed Business Information
ESTATES GAZETTE
151 WARDOUR STREET, LONDON W1F 8BN

First published in 2000 by Chandos Publishing (Oxford) Limited
This reformatted edition published by Estates Gazette in September 2002

ISBN 0 7282 0394 4

Printed in Great Britain

Contents

Preface

Buildings represent the largest capital investment that most businesses ever make and yet their use and function is often poorly understood by those responsible for their management. To an extent this is hardly surprising as buildings are extremely complicated pieces of equipment in their own right, and yet also contain a wide range of equally complicated pieces of equipment such as electrical systems. They are also controlled (both in their construction and use) by a host of overlapping regulatory requirements which are constantly being updated and amended. A building in use today may be anything from one to one hundred years old, and may have been built with a brick, concrete, stone, plastic or aluminium facade (to say nothing of the complexity of its internal structure). In such circumstances it is hardly surprising that the owners and tenants of commercial properties do not understand them as well as they would wish to.

This text is designed to provide a broad background for those who need to understand more about buildings and their use. It cannot aim at being a comprehensive guide (each chapter could be expanded to fill a large textbook) but will provide an introduction to the field for the non-professional.

It should also highlight one of the most important keys to the understanding of buildings, namely that no part of a building or anything in it exists in isolation, but is interlinked to a whole range of other issues. For this reason most building professionals – whether Surveyors, Architects or Facilities Managers – will have broad training and be able to provide advice on a wide range of different areas. This guide will not only help you understand and implement any advice you receive, but also help you understand exactly what it is you need to know before contacting a building professional, and so save you both time and money.

The Authors

Dr John Greed gained an LLB degree with honours at the University of Bristol in 1959 and qualified as a solicitor in 1963. In the 1960s he gained conveyancing experience in private practice and later with the Bristol & West Building Society. Since 1970 he has lectured in Land Law at the University of the West of England, Bristol. In 1998 he was awarded a PhD degree by the University of Reading.

Roger Heath, FRICS, FFB is a Senior Lecturer in Building Surveying at the University of the West of England, Bristol. A chartered building surveyor who spent 30 years working in both the public sector and private practice he now lectures in building performance, building pathology and construction law, and is co-author of *Understanding Housing Defects* published in 1998.

Dr Mark Steel studied Economics and Architecture at the University of Liverpool. He taught and conducted research programmes at both Liverpool and Manchester Universities before taking up a teaching and research post at the University of the West of England. His teaching and research interests include the economics of the construction and property industry and environmental economics.

Sue Wood qualified as an Architect after studying at Sheffield University; she then worked in that capacity for both local government and private practice before becoming a maintenance management consultant. Her research work includes studies for central government on stock condition surveys and access for people with disabilities. Currently, she is a Senior Lecturer at the University of the West of England, where she runs the MSc in Facilities Management.

All the authors teach courses for Building Surveyors, Facilities Managers, Quantity Surveyors, Architects and Construction Engineers in the Faculty of the Built Environment at the University of the West of England, Bristol BS16 1QY.

Chapter 1

The Provision and Use of Building Services

The efficient management of any business involves careful consideration of appropriate service installations. This will be equally important whether constructing a new building or assessing the provision of services within an existing building. In the latter case this may range from the installation of a completely new service or involve partial upgrading of, or extension to, an existing facility.

There are a number of underlying factors that influence the decisions of the building manager when considering any service installation. The following list sets out the more important of these factors:

- The amount of capital cost involved when making an initial choice for any new or upgraded service installation. The key concept is that of **life cycle costing**.
- The level of maintenance costs for any existing system. These may be rising or excessive due to inefficiencies within the existing system. Future maintenance costs should also be taken into account when making the initial decision on a new installation or the replacement of an existing one.
- An existing installation or any of its components may become worn out or inefficient due to age.
- Technological advances may result in existing components or a complete system becoming obsolete or inefficient in comparative terms. This sometimes happens even to relatively recent installations.
- Compliance with health and safety requirements can impose the need for review and change.
- The effect of:
  - changing commercial factors leading to increased or different service demands;
  - changing spatial needs;
  - changes imposed by statute;
  - changes required to meet insurance requirements.

This chapter discusses a number of commonly required services and sets out basic technical factors that will need to be considered if correct selection decisions are to be made by the building manager. Normally, such decisions should only be made after professional advice has been sought but some basic knowledge of those factors is useful in enabling the building manager to communicate ideas and issue a relevant brief to the service professional.

Main service installations

Water main

Water is supplied into a building by means of an underground service pipe which should be at a depth below ground level of 750 mm or greater. This is to avoid the freezing effect of ground frost during the winter months. There should be a water company stop cock in the highway close to the boundary at which the main enters the property (although in some older properties this may be found within the **curtilage**). On more recent installations, and where requested, a water meter (which incorporates a stop tap) would have been installed. These controlling devices mark the extent of the supply ownership and maintenance by the water company, ie it is the water company's responsibility to repair or replace pipework up to and including the meter.

Modern underground service pipes are of blue polyethylene but some older properties may still have lead water supply pipes. There is a risk of lead poisoning from such pipes. The government's Model Water Bye-laws of 1986 and subsequent water regulation prohibit the use of lead pipework in all new buildings and for any repairs to/replacement of existing pipes and fittings. If discovered they should be replaced as soon as possible.

The incoming main should enter the building via an underground duct before rising to just above the ground floor at which point there should be a combined stop tap and drain valve. This controls the flow of water to the complete building and enables the cold water system to be drained. It should be identified, properly maintained and made easily accessible for emergencies.

Electricity main

The electricity supply can be underground (commonly found in urban areas) or above ground (which is often the case in rural locations). In each case the supply will be taken to a main fuse and meter, normally positioned either outside of the building in a box or just inside the external point of entry. Both are the property of the electricity supply company. A connection will run from the company's meter to a **consumer control unit** (which is normally within the building). This type of unit is used for small and medium electrical loads. A more sophisticated type of control unit known as a **distribution board** is required for the heavier electrical loads used in factories and larger commercial buildings (discussion of which is outside of the content of this book). The consumer control unit and internal electrical distribution are discussed later in this chapter.

Gas main

A gas service pipe may enter a building above or below ground. In some cases it may be via an external meter box or the meter may be positioned within the building (this is more likely to be the case in older buildings). Where the main gas supply is taken up to the different levels of a multi-storey building before distribution via metering/sub-metering, it has to be contained within a protected and ventilated shaft. For safety purposes an isolating cock is positioned on the supply company's side of the meter.

The company's supply pipe may be of wrapped or coated steel, copper or unplasticised PVC, the last of which is now the most commonly used material. On the building user's side of the meter copper pipework is the norm, although older installations may have cast-iron, steel or lead pipework. All work on the gas installation must only be undertaken by either a gas company or CORGI (Council of Registered Gas Installers) approved service engineer.

Space heating installations

It is important that the working environment has an acceptable level of thermal comfort. Minimum temperature levels for the workplace are set by statutory regulation but the actual level of comfort experienced by the individual is a highly complex subject and depends upon a wide range of factors including the amount and type of clothing worn, the type of work activity involved and the level of ventilation or air movement. The modern space heating installation should provide fairly stable thermal conditions and a comfort level that reflects the buildings' use, and it achieves this by means of a mixture of efficient components and sophisticated controls. The system also needs to be regularly and appropriately maintained to ensure that it is always working at its optimum level of efficiency.

There are a number of factors that influence any decision on the choice of heating system to install. These include:

- **The availability of fuel and its cost**
  Natural gas has historically been the cheapest but is not available in many rural locations, although liquefied petroleum gas (which is more expensive and requires a storage tank) is sometimes used as an alternative. Oil similarly requires a storage facility but is relatively cheap. Coal is sometimes used but is dirtier, requires storage and is currently a more expensive fuel. Electricity is the cleanest fuel at point of use, is readily available (although an existing supply may need to be upgraded for any increased power load required) but is probably the most expensive fuel. However, at present the energy market is highly competitive and the suppliers of fuel and power are prepared to offer extremely good incentives and financial packages to secure customers, especially those who are likely to have a high energy consumption.

- **Capital costs**
  These are the costs of installation including the removal and replacement of any existing plant, infrastructure and components together with the cost of any associated builder's work.

- **Running and maintenance costs**
  These need to be carefully assessed and compared over the projected life of the installation.

- **Environmental implications**
  An assessment should be made of both the direct and indirect effects of the various systems under consideration, eg the level of carbon dioxide emissions which might be direct as from the flue of a gas heating boiler or indirect as with an electric heating system. With regard to the latter, it should also be borne in mind that, although electricity at the point of use is a clean fuel, high levels of carbon dioxide and other flue gases are discharged into the atmosphere at the power station.

- **The level of control required**
  With fuel costs tending to progressively rise and occupants requiring more flexible use of space as well as higher comfort levels, space (and hot water) heating systems are incorporating

increasingly sophisticated and sensitive controls. These devices include programmers to control time and prioritise functions of the system, thermostats to set temperature levels, pumps to accelerate the flow of water, diverter valves to prioritise the flow of the primary circuit between space or hot water use and frost thermostats to protect externally placed boilers. These controls may manage the complete system, separate zones within the installation or even individual spaces where appropriate.

Space heating installations fall into a number of different types of system as follows.

Hot water heating systems

These can be either:

- **a low temperature (low pressure) heating system** – a system in which the maximum temperature of the water is about 80°C. This type of system may operate by gravity (with larger diameter pipework) or with a pump (which enables the use of smaller diameter pipes, and is suitable for small and medium sized buildings); or

- **a high temperature (high pressure) heating system** – This operates at up to 200°C and is more appropriate for larger installations. It allows the sizes of heat emitters (see below) and pipe diameters to be reduced.

Hot water heating systems make use of heat emitters to provide the heat output to the building. The system is heated by a boiler fuelled by gas, oil, coal or electricity. There are a number of different types of heat emitters including:

- **Radiators**
  These are most commonly of pressed steel and may be single or double panels. Pressed steel radiators are prone to corrosion and it is advisable to incorporate a rust inhibiting additive in the circuit. Alternatively, consideration can be given to cast iron column radiators or cast aluminium alloy radiators (which are lighter than cast iron).

- **Convectors**
  These are based on air being warmed as it passes over a coil of hot water piping within a metal casing. Heat output is often increased by incorporating a fan in the emitter. The convectors

may be installed at low level (eg in offices) or at high level (eg in workshops).

- **Radiant panels**
  This system makes use of either high water temperatures to heat steel plates or strips or a gas burner to directly heat a metal duct adjoining a reflector plate to distribute the heat downwards. They are positioned at high level for safety reasons and are mostly used in industrial situations.

- **Underfloor heating**
  This consists of copper, mild steel or, most commonly in recent years (as it does not corrode), plastic pipe coils embedded in a solid floor. The water temperature involved is low (about 25°C) in order to prevent excessive expansion of the floor and any discomfort through foot contact. These systems achieve an acceptable level of thermal comfort although some of them tend to have high running costs.

Ducted warm air systems

These are most commonly heated by gas or electricity and are easiest installed in new buildings as part of the initial construction process. The warm air from the boiler or heating unit is circulated with the aid of a fan via a series of well insulated metal ducts positioned throughout the building, normally in floors, walls and ceilings. The ducts may be installed as a **stub duct system** or a **radial duct** system. With each it is necessary to provide grilles in doors to enable full circulation of the air and its eventual return to the heater.

Electric space heating systems

Although the running costs of electric space heating systems can be higher than those based on other fuels, these systems are frequently installed in both new and existing buildings because capital costs are lower, eg no large plant or extensive builder's work may be required. They are also quiet, easily maintained and have no risk of leaks or freezing.

The tariff structures of the electricity supply companies encourage the use of stored **off-peak** heating systems such as night storage heaters. However, in many situations, the use of direct heating appliances, such as fires and fan heaters, consuming more expensive but readily controllable standard **on-peak** electricity may be preferred.

Electrical space heating systems include:

- **Night storage heating**

  These may be achieved through a number of small individual units rated up to 3 kW in output which make use of heat-retentive blocks in a metal casing to store heat generated by off-peak electricity which is released throughout the working day. Input and output are controlled by separate thermostats on each unit. Alternatively, a single larger unit with an input loading of between 6 and 12 kW may be installed to provide the heating unit for a ducted warm air system (see above) which would be controlled by a room thermostat. The weakness of both systems is that the input load has to be decided before the beginning of each off-peak period, ie the day before the heat is required, and its release the day after may not precisely match the heating needs of the building.

- **Underfloor heating**

  Electric cables are encased in a solid concrete floor slab which then stores the heat generated from an off-peak supply and releases it throughout the day. Its major disadvantages are the inability to control the release of the heat when it is not required and high running costs.

- **Ceiling heating**

  This is worth considering if a building is particularly well insulated. Heating elements are installed between the joists or in a concrete slab together with appropriate insulation material. This type of system can be controlled by means of a thermostat and a timer and has a quick response time although it tends to have a high running cost.

- **Hot water thermal storage system**

  This makes use of off-peak electricity and a boiler or an immersion heater to heat water in a well insulated cylinder to as high a temperature as possible without generating steam (up to about 185°C). The stored hot water is then used to heat radiators and any hot water storage facility.

- **Individual heaters**

  In intermittently used buildings and areas where there is no need to provide continuous background heating it is often acceptable to provide on-peak direct heating that is used and controlled as needed. This is achieved by the use of a variety of fixed or portable appliances such as fires, oil-filled radiators, radiant heaters, convector heaters, fan heaters and tubular heaters. Most of these appliances are wall or floor fixed but some, such as radiant heaters, can be ceiling mounted.

Any assessment of a new or existing heating system needs to include consideration of the following:

- **Recent technological advances**
  The latest heat-producing appliances and system control devices, such as programmers and timers, make use of the latest technology. The **digital** variants of these controls tend to be much more sophisticated and have a greater range of functions than the **analogue** types. They are also more responsive to the building user's specific requirements. With many existing installations it is worth considering replacing the existing boiler and controls with those recently introduced because of the real increase in system efficiency and the accompanying savings in running costs.

  There have been radical developments with boiler technology over the last few years. A new generation of such heating appliances known as **condensing boilers** has been introduced. These burn 15 to 30 per cent less fuel than conventional designs and are also more efficient than the so-called **high-efficiency** boiler. Any boiler more than ten years old should be assessed for replacement as its efficiency will almost certainly not match the more recent designs. For example:

Boiler type	Efficiency
Conventional	70% to 80%
High-efficiency	80% to 85%
Condensing	85% to 90%

  In some cases the replacement of an old boiler has produced savings of up to 40 per cent of previous fuel bills.

  Greater use is now made of **thermostatic radiator valves** to remove dependence upon inefficient and insensitive centralised temperature control.

  Where an industrial or commercial business has access to quantities of low-temperature waste water or air, perhaps as a result of the process involved, it is worth considering the use of a heat pump. This can produce low-cost energy where there is a suitably cheap or free secondary energy source.

- **Zoning**
  This refers to the division of the building into separate zones of heating which can relate to varying use patterns, times, heating needs or tenancy arrangements. Each zone is individually controlled by means of its own programme and time controls, thermostatic temperature control and (where appropriate) metering.

Hot water installations

Hot water may be supplied via a central storage cylinder connected to a number of **draw-off points** or it may be more efficient to make use of independent **point-of-use water heaters**. These can be up to 25 per cent more efficient than centrally stored hot water especially if the demand is low and the distribution pipework is extensive. It is better to position draw-off points close to any storage cylinder and to each other so that long pipe runs with their associated heat losses are avoided.

Any hot water system should be installed to ensure that the **primary circuit** between the boiler and the cylinder is as short as possible. It is more efficient if this circuit is also fully pumped.

There are a number of different types of hot water cylinder including:

- **Direct cylinder**
  Water from the boiler is directly fed into the cylinder and then flows to the draw-off points. This is highly efficient but is only suitable where there is no space heating requirement especially in soft water areas. It is no longer installed because of the likelihood of furring in hard water areas but there are many such cylinders still in use.

- **Indirect cylinder**
  Water from the boiler flows through a fully sealed **heat exchanger** within the cylinder and indirectly heats the water. By separating the primary circuit and the drawn-off hot water this cylinder is suitable for hard water areas as there is minimal residual lime scale produced in the primary circuit.

- **Primatic cylinder**
  This is a type of indirect cylinder for small installations. Its advantage is that it reduces the number of ancillary tanks and pipes needed for the system.

- **Unvented hot-water storage systems**
  All of the above cylinders require a cold water storage tank and a considerable amount of sophisticated pipework. A fairly recent introduction, which has been permitted in the UK since 1986, is the unvented hot water system. This involves a hot water cylinder that is fed directly from the cold water main. The result is a pressurised hot water system which allows the use of smaller diameter pipes and fewer or no ancillary tanks. In order to meet stringent safety regulations governing such pressurised systems, each system must be manufactured as a complete proprietary package which has been approved by an authorised body. The package must include all necessary temperature and safety controls and be installed by an approved person.

The insulation of storage cylinders and any exposed pipework is essential in order to reduce heat losses. Modern hot water cylinders often have factory-applied insulating foam jackets and these are much more efficient than those with a jacket added at a later date. Pipe insulation can be added at any time but this is preferably carried out during initial installation.

It is the normal practice with hot water cylinders to install a 3 kW electric immersion heater. This provides the only source of heating for many electrical systems and a supplementary source with other fuel-heated systems that can be used if the primary source fails or is uneconomic in summer months. As with all electric heating, an immersion heater is expensive to run so it is advisable to link it to a timer control and set the heater temperature at a suitable level.

Much has been said in recent years about the apparent benefits of solar heating systems and it is true that they can make some contribution to any energy saving programme that may be initiated by a building manager. However, because of the limited amount of sunshine that the UK receives solar heating systems are somewhat restricted in application in this country, being more successful in providing hot water rather than space heating. It is normal to use such a system in tandem with a conventional water heating installation so that it can either boost the heat source or, in the sunnier seasons, fully provide hot water.

In smaller buildings and tenancies it is often sensible to consider point of use water heaters. For larger quantities of hot water (0.5 to 50 litres) a gas or electric thermal storage water heater will be more suitable. These may serve one or more draw-off points depending upon storage capacity and the gas variants will need to have a flue.

Cold water installations

As stated in the earlier section discussing main service installations, cold water installations were regulated by Model Water Bye-laws. Since 1 July 1999, The Water Supply (Water Fittings) Regulations 1999 have set standards for all new plumbing installations and for work on existing installations.

In the UK, especially the south and east where water resources are more scarce, it is usual to supply all appliances from tank storage within the building. The only exception to this is drinking water which should always be supplied direct from the water company's main. Where the pressure of the main is low or the building is tall it may be necessary to boost pressure with the aid of a pump.

The pipework of the modern installations is most commonly of copper although stainless steel and a variety of different plastics are also used. In the past steel and lead pipework has been commonly installed but now lead pipework is not permitted for any new work and should be replaced where it supplies drinking water as it presents a health hazard.

Smaller storage tanks are now manufactured in plastic while larger tanks tend to be of galvanised steel which may be sectionalised and assembled on site. All tanks should have a fixed cover or removable lid and be completely insulated if positioned in an unheated area. The same applies to all pipework in such areas of a building.

The flow of water (both cold and hot) through the system is controlled by a series of stop taps, stop valves and stop cocks. These are positioned to isolate the complete hot or cold water system or sections of it and any individual tanks and devices, eg boiler, pumps or draw-off points. They enable the system, or the appropriate section of it, to be shut down if there is an emergency or the need for maintenance or repair. They should be regularly checked to ensure that they are working properly and not a problem to use immediately if an emergency occurs.

Ventilation, extraction and air distribution systems

All buildings need to be ventilated in order to:

- provide a sufficient quantity and an acceptable quality of air to breathe;
- assist in any heating and cooling processes and in the reduction of unacceptable levels of **heat gain**;

- remove any traces of unhealthy or explosive gases, vapours and dust as well as body odours;
- remove any build-up of moisture in order to reduce the risk of condensation and associated mould growth.

It is also necessary to renew the air in each room of a building at frequent intervals in order to maintain a healthy environment. This frequency interval is expressed as the **air change rate**. In the UK the CIBSE Guide (see the useful reading list at the end of the report) sets out recommended hourly air change rates for a wide range of building/room uses (as well as other relevant air quality data).

Ventilation can be by means of one of two general approaches:

- Natural ventilation relies on natural air movement to ventilate, distribute and finally to exhaust air. This method is commonly chosen for many small to medium-sized commercial, retail and industrial buildings.
- Mechanical ventilation can be installed to achieve the same objectives. This may range from the *ad hoc* to the extremely sophisticated – from the use of simple fans to the installation of a complete air-conditioning system.

Each of these approaches is discussed in the following subsections.

Natural ventilation systems

Natural ventilation is selected because it is usually inexpensive to install in a building and cheap to use and maintain. It relies upon the difference between internal and external temperatures plus the effect of wind forces (which produce positive and negative pressures around a building) to provide the air movement within it. Traditionally, it has required no source of power, at its simplest relying on the manual opening and shutting of windows, ventilators and extract flues. In recent years there have been a number of increasingly sophisticated approaches introduced, ranging from **passive stack ventilation** to systems that make use of computer technology to centrally control and operate windows, ventilators and extractors in answer to the building user's need for fresh air and air movement.

Unfortunately, the climate of this country is extremely variable and unpredictable. The result is that the air quality, temperature and human comfort levels experienced in such buildings can be similarly adversely affected, often uncomfortably so. This can lead to poor human and/or equipment performance and affect the quality of any commercial or industrial production process.

It is possible, by careful design of the building and the service installations, to create an efficient and well balanced natural ventilation system that meets the needs of the building user. The design implications of such systems are complex and it can often be difficult to create a really efficient natural ventilation system in an existing building. Even so, increasing interest in the more advanced and controllable systems has been shown in recent years by users and designers of both small and large new and existing buildings. This in part reflects growing concerns about the energy efficiency and environmental impact of mechanical systems.

Mechanical ventilation, extraction and air distribution systems

Mechanical systems are used to provide full or partial ventilation as well as air distribution and extraction. There are three general approaches:

- natural inlet and mechanical extraction;
- mechanical inlet and natural extraction;
- mechanical inlet and mechanical extraction.

These systems rely upon a fan positioned at the input or output position, or in some systems at both, to produce desired air movement. The incoming air is often warmed in winter months to ensure that it is delivered at an acceptable temperature. At their simplest, one or more electric fans will merely blow fresh air into, or remove stale air from, a building, often being installed to serve specific rooms or areas.

More sophisticated systems make use of ducts to distribute the air throughout the building. Ducts are also commonly used on extraction systems which can be linked to the input system via a recirculation duct. When the air movement is forced into or out of the building it can result in a **plenum system**. With ducted systems it is necessary to provide either disposable filters (these use replaceable mats, panels or cartridges) or reusable filters (which have a cleaning mechanism to provide periodic dust removal) on the fresh air inlets and the recirculation air inlet. These ensure that all dust and other pollutants are removed, reducing the likelihood of **sick building syndrome** and respiratory problems.

The ducts are normally of galvanised steel but can also be supplied in plastic, aluminium or stainless steel. Their design and positioning needs to be carefully thought out as they can take up considerable floor space and can be difficult to hide in some buildings, especially those where the ducting cannot be placed above suspended ceilings or in vertical voids.

The efficiency of a ducted system can be increased by the addition of a **heat recovery system** or a **heat pump** which can reclaim heat from the exhausted air and other secondary heat sources. However, mechanical systems as a whole have limitations in application as they have difficulty in fully coping with internal heat gains. They are also powered by electricity which is not an efficient fuel source and contributes to overall carbon dioxide emissions.

Air-conditioning systems

Mechanical ventilation and extraction systems can be extremely sophisticated in their design and installation but are limited in terms of their control of the internal environment of a building. Many commercial, retail and manufacturing organisations require a fully controlled micro-climate and this can only be provided by an air-conditioning system. Often this is necessary because air quality of the highest standard is essential for the industrial or commercial processes taking place within the building. However, for some owners and occupiers it is more a matter of commercial prestige than for any other benefit, a belief that is created in part by the demands of the commercial property market.

The general principle behind the provision of such a system is to ensure that the internal climate is at its optimum for the comfort of the building's occupants and/or the operation of any machinery. The building is constructed with a hermetically sealed and highly insulated external envelope. This allows the air-conditioning system to totally control the internal temperature of the building as well as its air quality and humidity level. The exact balance will depend upon the controlling reason for the system, eg the comfort of the occupants, the demands of any commercial or industrial process, or the levels of air purity, humidity level and/or temperature needed for health or storage purposes.

There are a number of different approaches to the design of a system but these can be broadly divided between two air delivery mechanisms, the **all-air system** and the **air–water system**, each of which has a number of variants. In each type of air-conditioning system there are two essential components – a boiler to heat the air circulating within the building and a refrigeration plant to cool the air and control its humidity. There are also controls for temperature, air cleanliness and air movement throughout the building.

Whichever system is selected it needs to be designed to run as closely as possible to full load conditions in order to optimise both capital cost and energy efficiency. More recently installed systems often incorporate a heat recovery system in the extract air in order increase energy efficiency. The design also needs to avoid over-estimation of the cooling and heating requirements of the building, a common error that results in a system that is only needed to run intermittently. This leaves plant to stand idle for long periods and expend energy inefficiently on repeated start-up processes.

It is normal practice to air-condition a complete building. Division of a building into a number of separate individually controlled zones to meet different user demands is possible with some types of system. For example, the **variable air volume (VAV)** system, popular in the 1980s, readily allows cellular office formation. On the other hand, the **chilled beam** system, which was introduced into the UK in the 1990s, is more restrictive and offers less flexibility in spatial design. However, it has better humidity control and is cheaper to run and maintain than the VAV system.

With existing buildings it is usually too difficult and probably not cost-effective to attempt to fully air-condition the entire building unless the work is undertaken as part of a major refurbishment scheme. However, it is possible to create air-conditioned rooms or areas within an existing building by hermetically sealing the designated area and installing a **packaged plant** in a suitable service area (often an external flat roof).

Particular problems that impact upon both new and existing buildings are:

- although light in weight a large volume of space is needed for the air treatment plant (it is often placed at roof level because of the space factor and because air input and air exhaust requirements can be readily met);
- the need to insert large amounts of ducting for air movement around the building.

In recent years a number of questions have been raised concerning the financial viability and health and environmental effects of air-conditioning systems. They have been found to be expensive in terms of energy consumption, requiring up to 30 per cent of the total energy cost of an air-conditioned building. They are known to be a contributory factor in outbreaks of legionnella and **sick building syndrome** as well as contributing to problems with asthma in some people. Many existing systems demand frequent and careful cleaning and sterilisation of the water spray chambers that are incorporated to control humidity, although in newer systems humidity levels are maintained by steam injection which reduces problems of hygiene. Older systems also make use in their refrigeration processes of chlorofluorocarbons (CFCs), the venting of which directly harms the ozone layer. This problem is now avoided by the use of the latest **absorption cycle air-conditioning systems** which allow cooling without the use of CFCs. However, such concerns have led many designers and building users to consider alternative means of controlling the internal environment of a building including a return to natural ventilation or the use of a **passive stack ventilation system**.

Electrical distribution and power systems

As discussed earlier in this chapter the electricity main belongs to the supply company as far as the meter position. The building user's control over the electrical system occurs at the **distribution board** (commonly known as a **consumer control unit** in smaller systems) which is normally positioned close to the meter.

In smaller commercial and other premises electricity is distributed by means of a number of **ring mains** each connected to the consumer control unit. There are limits to the floor area that each ring main can serve and this often results in further division of each type of power need into a number of separate ring mains, eg one for each floor or part of a building where it is very large. Similar division is also recommended if zones of use or separate tenancy areas are created.

A consumer control unit incorporates a main control switch and a number of either rewirable fuses or, in modern units, **miniature circuit breakers (MCBs)** – one for each ring main of which there may be up to twelve. The former are the cheaper, simpler and traditional means of ensuring that the supply is broken if a fault or overload situation develops. However, they can deteriorate in use and can be subject to abuse or tampering resulting in a highly dangerous circuit overload. This has led to the introduction of the MCB which cannot be overridden. It is now common practice (in fact highly desirable in terms of safety) also to incorporate an earth leakage circuit breaker (ELCB) in a consumer control unit to protect either all internal circuits or at least those considered to be of greater potential risk, eg power circuits.

Industrial and larger commercial buildings normally require a more sophisticated distribution system in order to handle the higher electrical loads involved. The system is controlled by a distribution board and associated switchgear and often includes a series of internal mains and sub-mains serving the various user needs. The internal mains are connected to further distribution boards and switchgear for control of each sub-main. The individual circuits in these larger systems are known as **radial circuits**.

In buildings where there is multiple occupation there should be a separate sub-mains to each individually tenanted area. Each tenancy area should have either its own meter or sub-meter together with a further distribution board or consumer control unit (as described above) controlling the various ring mains or radial circuits.

Lighting systems

In a factory lighting may account for up to 15 per cent of the energy consumed. This percentage increases to 20 per cent in a modern commercial building. A properly designed and maintained lighting installation can contribute significant savings towards the running costs of a building, eg a dirty lamp or fitting can lose up to 80 per cent of its effective light, inadequately controlled lights can remain on when the building is unoccupied, **heat gain** from lighting can adversely affect ventilation and heating systems. Where more sophisticated control is sought consideration may be given to a lighting management system into which the needs of the occupier are specifically programmed. This can be linked to a building management system (BMS) – discussed at the end of this chapter.

The level of lighting and the type of installation both depend on a number of factors including:

- the type of work or retailing taking place;
- the office or work/sales space configuration, eg open plan, individual rooms, offices or work/sales areas;
- the amount of natural light (daylight) available;
- the level of task lighting required at desk, screen or work/sales bench plus background general illumination;
- the occupancy pattern, eg intermittent, variable or full;
- any demands imposed by security needs;

- the need to meet statutory requirements, eg those for health and safety and fire and means of escape.

A building may have one or more lighting circuits. Each floor or separate tenancy area on any floor should have its own lighting circuit. In larger buildings the individual floor areas, especially when open plan, should be subdivided into several separately controlled lighting zones in order to allow for local control of work areas and circulation spaces. Separate circuits are required for emergency lighting systems and are recommended for any security and external lighting.

Recent advances in technology have resulted in the availability of controlling devices and other components that offer greater flexibility of use and increase the efficiency of the installation. These include:

- Low-energy fittings such as **compact fluorescent lamps (CFLs)** – a type of light bulb. Although higher in capital cost than the more normally used tungsten filament bulb, these last up to eight times longer.
- The latest fluorescent **luminaires** normally contain more efficient reflectors resulting in less fittings being required. The inclusion of a high-frequency **ballast** can further increase efficiency by saving up to 15–20 per cent of the energy needed for the luminaire.
- Timing devices and/or occupancy sensors for intermittently used areas and rooms. These are particularly useful for circulation spaces, washrooms and toilets.
- The use of daylight sensors that automatically enable an optimum mix of natural and artificial light to be achieved. Internally, the use of natural light can be enhanced by regular internal and external cleaning of windows. The control of external lighting by such sensors ensures an appropriate level of lighting for safety and security reasons at all times of day.
- Manually operated dimmer switches can be installed to adjust the level of artificial light. However, this type of control is less efficient than a daylight sensor in achieving a balance with natural light.

Lift systems

In multi-storeyed buildings it is sensible to consider the installation of one or more lifts to ease access for people and goods to the upper storeys. Part M of the **Building Regulations** now requires all new commercial, retail and industrial buildings and any extension to an existing building of these types of use to include the provision of access for disabled persons to all floor levels. The installation of a lift can ensure compliance with the Regulations. The exact number of lifts installed depends upon a range of factors including the number of potential passengers or the amount of goods to be transported. In larger buildings **banks of lifts** are often installed to handle the high numbers of passengers involved.

Most lifts are installed for either passenger or goods movement although some are specifically required to handle both.

- **Passenger lifts**
  These can be designed to meet a range of variable criteria depending upon the building owner's or occupier's specific requirements. These criteria include:
  - size as lifts are manufactured in a range of capacities;
  - quality of finish which can be from functional to prestigious;
  - lift control which can be automatic or involve attendant operation;
  - travel speed which can range from slow to fast.

- **Disabled access lifts**
  These are lifts of lightweight construction and slower operating speeds that are specifically designed to transport disabled people. They are not meant for use by a large volume of people.

- **Goods lifts**
  These carry bulkier or heavier goods between floors and are finished in hard-wearing but utilitarian materials. This type of lift operates relatively slowly.

- **Service lifts**
  These are small goods only lifts. They are used, for example, to deliver food where a kitchen and a restaurant or a dining room are on separate floors. They may be hand-powered, or electrically-operated for heavier loads (up to 500 kilograms).

The operation of a lift is based upon several alternative power sources:

- **Hydraulic lifts**
  These are cheaper to install but more expensive to run than electric lifts. However, they are relatively easy to maintain. They are installed where the maximum height travelled is no greater than 18–21 metres. The lift travel speed is moderate, making

them suitable for goods transportation and the movement of disabled/elderly persons.

- **Electric lifts**

  These can operate at much greater speeds than hydraulic lifts making them highly suitable for the carrying of passengers. They require more vertical and horizontal space than hydraulic lifts to accommodate the necessary plant. They also impose greater demands in structural terms on any supporting construction, making their installation inappropriate for many existing buildings where hydraulic lifts are generally better suited, although some smaller electric lifts do have their own self-supporting framework.

- **Hand-operated lifts**

  These are small hand-powered lifts used to carry light loads such as food and similar goods – the so-called service lift. The maximum amount of load would not normally exceed 100 kilograms and the mode of power is an endless rope or chain.

The decision to install a lift needs to take into account a number of key factors:

- the amount of floor space available for the lift, its operating machinery and the access lobbies on each floor;
- the intended passenger or goods capacity;
- the travel speed of the lift.

A decision also needs to be made on the type of control system that is to be installed. This is based upon the processing of calls for a lift at each landing and the prioritising of the selected destination in the lift car. This is carried out by one of the following methods:

- **Single automatic push-button**

  In this, the simplest system, a single call button is provided on each landing with destination buttons in the lift car. Control is limited to one call at a time operating the lift which will not then respond to any other control button until it has reached the targeted level and rested for a few seconds.

- **Collective control**

  Up and down buttons are provided on all landings and destination buttons in the lift. Calls are dealt with only in the direction that the lift is travelling. This produces slow response times.

- **Down-collective control**

  This is suitable for buildings where the majority of movement is between the ground floor and other floors with little or no movement between floors, eg a tenanted building. The system prioritises up calls from the ground floor and down calls in the order of landing level (highest first).

- **Group collective control**
  This allows a **bank of lifts** (up to a maximum of four) to be grouped in a controlled group. The closest lift or the first moving in the desired direction will respond to the call.

- **Group supervisory control**
  Banks of lifts handling large volumes of traffic are controlled by a computer that prioritises the service in answer to traffic demands. It also helps to minimise uneven service and reduce waiting times.

- **Attendant control**
  This is still used in some retail premises but is less common elsewhere. The lift can be operated as directed by the attendant. Some lifts are fitted with dual controls that allow normal automatic control by one of the methods set out above while allowing this to be overridden as required for attendant control.

Further factors that need consideration include:

- **Fire protection**
  The vertical lift shaft offers an easy route for the spread of fire and smoke through a building. This means that any installation must meet high levels of fire protection provision to prevent these hazards spreading. The lift shaft and the lift door openings at all levels must be of non-combustible materials and both fire and smoke resistant. All landings must be similarly enclosed. A lift cannot be used as a means of escape in the event of a fire. This means that there must be at least one suitable staircase available for this purpose.

- **Sound insulation**
  The operation of the lift and the accompanying plant creates considerable noise. Any installation must be designed and constructed so that the impact of noise on adjoining areas of the building is reduced to a minimum.

- **Vandalism**
  This can be a problem in lifts with uncontrolled access. Past experience of lift operators would indicate that the use of toughened glass mirrors on all vertical surfaces within the lift car reduces the incidence of vandalism. All other surfaces and the controls also need to be vandal resistant.

- **Emergencies**
  Sometimes the lift may break down in mid-operation. This may automatically trigger an alarm at a suitable control office or there may be a manual alarm button in the car. The lift car can be provided with a two-way telephone system linking it to the control office.

Lift manufacturers normally offer a design and installation service for their own lifts. However, it is common practice for the building manager (or a professional consultant) to arrange separately for all of the related builder's work (eg forming new walls, door openings and lobbies) and for the alteration of any services (eg extending the electrical supply). This includes both the design and construction processes necessary to enable these ancillary works to be completed as well as any coordination between the lift manufacturer/installer and the other parties.

Fire detection and fighting systems

Fire is a potential hazard in all buildings. The risk of fire can be increased by a number of factors including:

- the particular use of the building, eg the storage of flammable goods;
- the type of construction and the materials used in that construction, eg combustible (such as plastic cladding) rather than non-combustible (such as steel sheeting);
- deterioration of key services, especially electrics or gas, due to age;
- lack of regular maintenance of key services.

There is a considerable amount of legislation to regulate the design, construction and use of all buildings in terms of fire prevention and control. The Building Regulations (which are frequently updated) set design and construction standards for new building works and alterations to existing buildings. Part B deals with fire safety in buildings and makes reference to a number of British Standards. Various Acts of Parliament cover the actual use of commercial, retail and industrial buildings. The most important of these is the Fire Precautions Act 1971 which requires users of such buildings to meet prescribed standards of fire safety in order to obtain a fire certificate from the local fire authority.

Past legislation in the UK was very prescriptive with regard to fire protection and was heavily criticised by both designers and building users as it did not encourage innovative design. This has changed in the 1990s and the latest Building Regulations permit very flexible design interpretation of their requirements without reducing the regulatory standards applied, eg **fire engineering**.

The underlying priority of UK fire legislation is to save life. Historically, it has attempted to do this by:

- ensuring adequate means of escape from the building for any occupants;
- reducing the spread of fire within the building and between adjoining buildings;
- regulating the use, and in some cases the contents, of a building.

To these can now be added:

- providing access for fire-fighting vehicles.

The general aim is to provide early warning and speedy evacuation of the occupants of the building in the event of a fire. This is linked to preventing the spread of fire which makes sense as more people are killed from inhalation of smoke and toxic gases than by heat and flames. It should also be noted that although it is the primary purpose of the legislators and the fire service to protect and save life the Association of British Insurers feels that any protection measures should also take into account the need to save the fabric and contents of the building.

There are two general approaches to the provision of fire protect-ion, each of which are discussed in the following subsections of this chapter. All buildings must incorporate **passive fire protection** measures together with as many of the **active fire protection** measures as are considered appropriate for the safety of the occupants and the building.

Passive fire protection

A detailed discussion of the measures involved in passive fire protection is outside the terms of this book. However, the brief principles are as follows:

- The design must divide the building into a number of **compartments**.
- Means of escape routes from each compartment are similarly formed, each route leading to a **place of safety** outside of the building.

• Non-combustible or suitably treated materials are used where appropriate throughout the building or area of refurbishment to reduce the spread of flame.

Active fire protection

There are a number of individual active fire protection measures that can be installed. It is normal to link a number of different measures together to form a complete fire detection and warning system. This can be further linked to a fire-fighting installation such as a sprinkler system.

Fire detection systems

These comprise automatic fire detection sensors installed at high-risk points throughout a building together with audible warning devices and a control unit. They can be linked to a fire-fighting system such as sprinklers.

- **Detection sensors**
  There are a great many different devices available, making use of a variety of detection technologies. They all detect one of the following three effects of any fire – smoke, heat or flames.
  - *Smoke detector*
    The most commonly installed type of detector, this detects any build-up of smoke in an enclosed room or area. It can be extremely sensitive.
  - *Heat detector*
    This is installed where the presence of smoke in a room occurs as a result of the normal activities taking place, eg in a kitchen or metal forge, making it necessary to install another type of fire detection device.
  - *Flame detector*
    This is a detection device that is installed in external areas where smoke and heat are readily dissipated and do not trigger an alarm quickly enough. A flame detector can be used in these situations although it needs to be recognised that its effectiveness can be negated by smoke obscuring any flames.

- **Audible warning devices**
  These consist of bells, klaxons or hooters and are positioned so that they can be heard in all rooms and areas within the building.

Once set off they should remain on until physically turned off at the control unit. This ensures that the building is properly evacuated and then checked to see if the alarm is real or false. They may also be linked to an automatic warning system at the local fire station.

- **Control unit**
  This is installed at a suitable position within the building, normally close to or in the main entrance or reception area. If the building has a building management system (BMS) (see later in this chapter), the control unit will usually be integrated into it. Most buildings will have the detection system divided into zones so that it is easier to identify the source of any alarm at the control unit. The alarm system on the other hand will be set off throughout the whole of the protected building.

Fire fighting installations

- **Sprinkler systems**
  A network of dedicated pipework is distributed throughout the building or area concerned to serve sprinklers at or just below ceiling level. The pipework can be a **wet system** or a **dry system**. A variety of different heat-sensitive sprinkler heads is available. The exact operation of each head depends upon the level of heat sensitivity required and the spray pattern of the particular head selected. The area covered by one head is determined by the water pressure feeding it as well as the type of head. It ranges from about 7.5 to 21 square metres, the higher the likely fire risk the smaller the coverage area of each head installed.

  Sprinkler systems are suitable for all types of commercial, retail and industrial premises but they are viewed with some concern by occupiers as the purpose of their operation is to automatically drench any fire with water. This will put out the fire very efficiently but can have the added effect of causing considerable water damage to the building and its contents. Sprinklers which deliver a fine mist rather than water droplets have been found to be as effective, if not more so, than the latter without the need for a large volume of water.

- **Hose reels**
  These are sometimes installed to allow occupants to tackle a fire while awaiting the arrival of the fire brigade. The hose reels are positioned on each floor close to escape stairwells to avoid

overexposing users to danger. The fire services have mixed feelings about the provision of these and other pieces of fire-fighting equipment as they can encourage people to stay too long in a building in dangerous circumstances rather than immediately evacuate it.

- **Wet risers and dry risers**
It is common practice in taller and larger buildings to install one or more 100 mm or larger diameter wet risers or dry risers to assist the fire service. These risers are not for any other purpose than to enable the fire service to attach its own hoses to a water supply at the valved outlet on each floor level. They are positioned in a stairwell or landing. The risers speed up the fire-fighting process and overcome any problems caused by distance limitations of the apparatus on a fire tender.

Smoke ventilation

Many single-storey buildings, especially those with large open work spaces or circulation areas including atria, make use of automatic fire ventilation. This comprises one or more roof ventilators that automatically open when triggered by the fire detection system to remove heat, smoke and toxic gases from the building. This reduces the build-up of the fire and aids visibility, initially for those escaping and then for the fire services. The ventilator may also be used for normal ventilation. Smoke ventilation can also be achieved by means of window actuators linked to the fire alarm system or, in multi-storeyed buildings, by specifically designed mechanical extraction.

Security systems

The building manager needs to consider the security of a building for a number of potential problems. These include theft, vandalism and unauthorised access. It may be possible to prevent the last problem solely by the use of **passive security measures** at the perimeter of the building or land enclosing it. Such measures may also provide the means of preventing vandalism and theft but these two problems are more difficult to deal with and counter-measures will almost certainly involve the use of **active security measures**.

Passive security measures

These are used to prevent unauthorised access to land and buildings in general, or to more sensitive external or internal areas. A detailed discussion of the measures involved is outside the terms of this book. Briefly they include:

- the provision of security walls, screens and fencing;
- the provision only of controlled entry points on the perimeter of land, in a building or at a security area. All other potential entry points, such as rooflights, windows and uncontrolled secondary doors, are provided with appropriate security devices, eg window restrictors, automatic door closers and self-locking devices, emergency crash bars on fire exits.

Active security measures

There are a number of active devices and systems available, some of the more common being listed below. They may be used individually but it is more usual for the security designer to incorporate a mixture of passive security measures and active security measures into the selected system.

- **Detection sensors**
  These devices detect movement and may be positioned internally and/or externally. They may be installed singly but usually there are a number of detectors positioned throughout a building or protected area forming an integrated system linked to audible warning devices and a control panel. The audible warning may be inside and/or outside of the building and the system may be connected to the nearest police station or the control centre of a private security company.

  The system will be operated by mains electricity but should have battery back-up. A complete system may include one or more of several types of device. The following list gives a general indication of some of the approaches that may be included:

  - contacts and micro-switches on doors and windows which will trigger the alarm if opened and which may be magnetic or mechanical in operation;
  - taut wiring systems which can be installed in windows, screens, walls, floors and ceilings and will activate the alarm if disturbed;

- infra-red detectors which set off the alarm (or turn on a light) if an invisible beam is broken;
- pressure-operated systems which are activated by the change in air pressure when a door or window is opened;
- pressure mats which trigger an alarm when stepped upon;
- vibration-operated systems which may be linked mechanically to a sensitive spring-leaf detector or electronically to a microphone;
- ultrasonic detectors which are triggered by changes in the frequency of sound waves as a result of movement.

- **Panic or alarm buttons**
  These are installed where it is important to trigger the alarm system due to a security incident when the building or secure area is in authorised use.

- **Closed circuit television (CCTV)**
  This enables centrally located monitoring of movement into, through and out of a building or area. It may be used in conjunction with an electronic locking system to control access and is often linked to a video recording system.

- **Access control**
  At its simplest this can be achieved by the use of suitable keys limiting desired access to authorised personnel. More sophisticated methods of access control include a number of electronically controlled devices such as digital number pads and coded card readers, both of which can allow varying levels of authorised access at a controlled door. There has also been much research into the use of processes that identify an authorised person from his/her individual physical characteristics, eg handprint, voice pattern or eye details. Advances in such technology mean that future controls over access will become even more highly sophisticated and individually tailored.

Building management systems (BMS)

The trend towards centrally and continually monitored services performing within a fully controlled internal environment has resulted in the building management system. Originally known as a building and energy management system (BEMS) it is an integrated approach that makes use of the latest microcomputer-based technology to manage all the service installations within a building. By this means it is possible to develop and ensure the performance of sophisticated strategies for energy efficiency (full and flexible control of heating, ventilating, air-conditioning and lighting of the building) and other service requirements such as fire alarm, security and access control.

The use of interactive software programs means that although the individual services are physically separate their use and management can be integrated in any way and to any level that the building manager desires. The BMS can also supply information needed to assist in the making of future management decisions, eg installation performance data and incident logs as well as calculations such as an energy audit.

The BMS is based on a computer that is linked to appropriately positioned sensors that continuously monitor and control the numerous functions of all the individual service installations. The sensors are linked to the computer by cable although there has been some recent research by the Building Research Establishment and others into the use of cordless sensors.

The BMS requires the presence of a minimal number of highly experienced engineering personnel at a central work station to monitor and oversee the complete operation of all services. They constantly interpret the feed-back information and adjust the system to ensure that the individual service installations are operating at an optimum level of efficiency. These skilled field engineers also ensure that all of the plant for each service installation is maintained to the highest standards, an essential prerequisite (along with good initial design of both the building and the plant) if the BMS is to be successful.

Chapter 2

Property and the Law

What parts of the Law are relevant to a property manager? That depends on what the particular property manager does. And what property managers do varies infinitely, depending largely on what property is being managed. Consider, for example:

- a manager in charge of a motorway service station;
- the estates manager of a building society who is responsible for the society's 1960s high-rise head office and a string of branch offices;
- the maintenance team of a university campus where the science faculty uses radioactive materials and the Library has irreplaceable medieval manuscripts in store;
- a member of a commercial firm who is told, 'We're delegating office maintenance to you because there's no one else to do it.'

All of these are property managers, although they all have different training, qualifications and experience. Some of them will have some knowledge of law; some will not. The aim of this chapter is that it should be useful both to those who have such knowledge and those who do not.

Though the types of law involved in property management are as varied as the types of property manager, there are certain categories of law which would be relevant to the managers in all the above examples. All of them would benefit from an acquaintance with the basic legal rules about contracts; any of them may find themselves having to consider the law of tort (torts being 'civil wrongs') such as the tort of negligence if someone is injured on their premises; and some knowledge of how the legal system and the courts are organised may be useful to them all. This chapter deals with these general matters.

It follows that this account is bound to be generalised and should not be used as a substitute for professional legal advice. On the contrary, it is hoped that this chapter will send the property manager in search of such advice in situations where he or she would otherwise not have realised the need for it.

The courts

The law (and the courts) can be divided into civil and criminal. Criminal law is primarily to punish – or to reform – the offender, while a major function of civil law is to compensate the victim.

Criminal courts

Small criminal cases are heard in the magistrates' court, while serious cases are heard in front of Judge and jury in the Crown Court. There is a middle category of cases triable either way – the defendant is given the choice of having the case dealt with summarily (ie by the magistrates) or at the Crown Court. All solicitors have the **right of audience** in the magistrates' court, but most solicitors have no such right in the Crown Court. Barristers have the right of audience in all courts.

Civil courts

The fact that someone accidentally or even deliberately causes you to suffer a loss or injury does not entitle you to a remedy unless you can bring the case within the boundaries of some legally recognised wrong – such as a breach of contract, or breach of trust by a trustee, or one of the torts such as negligence, nuisance, trespass, libel and slander. (All of these are civil law, dealt with in the civil courts.)

Cases in which the amount claimed exceeds £50,000 go to the High Court, but smaller cases go to the County Court. (There is a County Court in most large towns, not just one per county.) All solicitors have the right of audience in the County Court, but most have no such right in the High Court, so if you are suing for more than £50,000, your solicitor will have to instruct a barrister to argue the case in the court. If the sum does not exceed £5,000, the case is likely to be dealt with by the County Court Judge's assistant, the District Judge, in the branch of the County Court known as the small claims court.

The court you are most likely to come across is the County Court. Maybe you will be suing someone for tort, or for breach of contract; or maybe someone fell down your office stairs and is suing your firm for compensation for the tort of negligence on the grounds that the stairs or the lights were not properly maintained; or maybe you are appearing as a witness (possibly an expert witness because of your specialised knowledge of buildings) in someone else's case.

And sometimes you may have to go to a criminal court – as a witness, it would be hoped, not as a defendant!

Giving evidence

The procedure for giving evidence, whether it is in a criminal court or a civil court, will follow a set pattern: (1) the oath; (2) the examination; (3) the cross-examination; and (4) sometimes a re-examination.

1 **The oath**

The witness is called into court (for he or she will have been waiting outside, because witnesses are not allowed to hear what previous witnesses say) and goes up the steps into the witness box. The usher hands the witness a copy of the New Testament (or Old Testament for a Jewish witness, Qu'ran for a Muslim witness, etc) and the witness swears the oath. The normal oath is, 'I swear by Almighty God that the evidence I shall give shall be the truth, the whole truth, and nothing but the truth'. A witness who does not wish to swear an oath is permitted to make an affirmation: 'I solemnly and sincerely affirm that the evidence ... etc'.

2 **The examination**

A witness 'thrown in at the deep end' to give his or her evidence would be likely either to get stage fright or to waste the court's time with irrelevant details: so the solicitor or barrister acting for the party who called the witness to court will ask questions to draw out the relevant facts. 'Where were you on the evening of 2nd February?' 'What did you see?' Note that none of these is a **leading question**. Such questions, which would put answers into the mind of the witness, are not allowed.

3 **The cross-examination**

The solicitor or barrister acting for the other party now stands up, and the witness must be ready for a possible rough ride, for it is this lawyer's duty to probe any weak points in the evidence which the witness has given. Here, leading questions are allowed. 'It was February and it was snowing: lots of people wear balaclavas in such weather, don't they?' 'So you couldn't see his face?' 'And from where you were, you could not clearly see whether he was holding a pistol or a telescopic umbrella, could you?' The cross-examiner may show that the witness is forgetful, uncertain or confused, and may show that an expert witness seems less expert than at first appeared.

4 The re-examination

If new points, not mentioned in the examination, came out in the cross-examination, there can be a re-examination (with no leading questions) to clarify these points. The questioning will go no further. There is no re-cross-examination.

Letters written in the run-up to a court case are often headed 'Without Prejudice'. This phrase means that the party receiving the letter cannot generally use it in evidence. Another useful phrase (often used in negotiations for the sale of land) is 'Subject to Contract', meaning, 'This document is not a contract, it is no more than a negotiation'.

Appeals

A person who loses a case may wish to appeal against the decision. Appeals are to the Court of Appeal (or sometimes to the Divisional Court) and on a matter of general public importance there can be a further appeal to the House of Lords. The House of Lords in this context means a body of senior judges (usually five of them) who are Law Lords. There is generally no appeal against a House of Lords decision.

The law

The two main sources of English law are legislation and precedent.

- **Legislation**

  This consists of statutes (Acts of Parliament) and delegated legislation. Statutes may be primarily on criminal law, such as the Theft Act 1968, or may be on civil law, such as the Law of Property Act 1925, which lays down the present system of freehold and leasehold land for England and Wales. (Scotland has a different land law system.) 'Delegated legislation' is law made by an authorised body (such as a government minister or a local council) using power delegated to it by Parliament. Examples of delegated legislation include by-laws made by local councils, Construction and Use Regulations about the size and weight of lorries, and the Building Regulations about the standard of materials and workmanship required in buildings.

- **Precedent**

  This is case-law. The idea of precedent is that a judge is not allowed to contradict a principle that has been laid down in the judgment of a previous case. This increases the certainty of the law (because claimants can often be told, 'There is a previous case on this point, and so yours will be decided the same way') but it can result in injustice which the judge has no power to prevent. The House of Lords is the only court that is not bound to follow precedent. Some of the laws discussed below date back over 100 years but are still cited every day in the courts.

Half the battle in understanding law is in understanding the way lawyers think. The courts try to give 'justice within the law'. When a case comes to court, the question to be decided is not merely, 'What is a fair and just answer?' but 'Has there been an earlier case in which this point of law has previously arisen?' The judge in the later case is not allowed to contradict a point of law decided in a previous case. That is what is meant by 'binding precedent'. Let us take some examples from the law of contract and look at the cases of *Cundy* v *Lindsay* and *King's Norton Metal Co Ltd* v *Edridge Merrett & Co Ltd*, and then apply them to a modern property management situation. Although these cases are over a hundred years old they are still highly relevant today, because if they are cited as 'binding precedents' they will determine the outcome of any case you are involved in.

In *Cundy* v *Lindsay* (1878)[1] a manufacturer (Lindsay & Co) was in the habit of supplying goods on credit to its regular customers, one of these being a firm called Blenkiron. Lindsays then received an order from someone named Blenkarn, who had set up business in the same street as Blenkiron. They sent the goods on credit, thinking they were dealing with Blenkiron. Blenkarn did not pay for the goods, but he sold them to Cundy, who paid Blenkarn for them. Lindsays claimed the goods back, as they had not been paid for them. Lindsays won, as the mistake of identity, mistaking Blenkarn for Blenkiron, rendered their contract with Blenkarn void. Therefore *ownership* of the goods did not pass to Blenkarn (though *possession* did) and so he had no ownership to pass on to Cundy. Therefore Cundy was not the owner: he had to return the goods to Lindsays and was left with nothing but a right of suing Blenkarn.

In *King's Norton Metal Co Ltd* v *Edridge Merrett & Co Ltd* (1897)[2] the King's Norton Metal Co received an order for goods, on rather impressive notepaper headed 'Hallam & Co.' They sent the goods, and were paid. They received a second order and sent the goods, and were not paid: and on investigation they found that Hallam &

Co did not exist except in the imagination of a crook called Wallis, who had had the notepaper printed and was using it to obtain goods on credit. Meanwhile, Wallis had sold the goods to Edridge Merrett & Co Ltd, which had paid Wallis for them. (So, just as in *Cundy* v *Lindsay*, the position was that 'A' had sold goods to 'B', who had not paid for them, and 'B' had then sold them to 'C' who had paid 'B' for them, and 'B' had then absconded with the money.) The King's Norton firm claimed the goods back, as it had not been paid for them. If this is the same point as in *Cundy* v *Lindsay*, the King's Norton firm must win, because the court cannot contradict the rule laid down in the previous case. But the court concluded that it is not the same point. In *Cundy* v *Lindsay* there had been a mistake of identity (Blenkarn for Blenkiron). In this case it was not so. They thought they were dealing with a purchaser not known to them (except that they knew that last time, their bill had been paid) and there was no mistake, for that is exactly who they were dealing with, and he turned out to be a crook operating under a false name. They had trusted someone who proved to be unreliable: but they had not mistaken that person for some other person well known to them, as the vendors in *Cundy* v *Lindsay* had done. So the contract to sell to Hallam & Co (alias Wallis) was not void: so ownership of the goods had passed to Wallis (for ownership passes when the goods are delivered, even if not paid for) and so Wallis could and did pass the ownership on to Edridge Merrett & Co Ltd who were therefore entitled to keep the goods, leaving the King's Norton firm with nothing but the right to sue Wallis.

The practical implications of these cases of 'binding precedent' are clear. Suppose your firm has bought office furniture from a firm, Expert Ltd. Your firm has paid Expert Ltd, but now the manufacturer demands the goods back, because it has not been paid by Expert Ltd. Whether your firm will have to hand back the goods does not depend on the justice of the case, nor on anything you have done. It depends on the next contract down the chain, over which your firm had no control. If the manufacturer sold to Expert Ltd as an ordinary business risk, the situation is like that in the *King's Norton* case, in which the purchaser was able to keep the goods. But if the manufacturer can show that it only sold to Expert Ltd because it mistook it for its trusted regular customer Export Ltd, *that* contract was void for mistake of identity as in *Cundy* v *Lindsay*, and so Expert Ltd had no ownership to pass on to your firm and the goods will have to be handed back. The outcome of the case depends on which of these two nineteenth-century precedent cases (neither of which was about property management) the court will have to follow. The point is these cases (and other even older ones) laid down a general legal principle, that a mistake going to the heart of a contract makes that contract void, and *that* principle applies henceforth to all contracts for all transactions. And that includes, of course, all property management contracts.

Contract

A contract is a legally enforceable agreement. Its essential feature is that an offer has been accepted *in return for something*. The offer might be to sell or to buy something or to do something. For example, I could offer to sell you my car in return for £5,000. Or you might approach me and offer to buy my car for £5,000. Or there might be an offer to perform services, as when someone offers (perhaps by tender) to do certain work for you in return for a certain payment. If the offer is accepted, that is a contract. There is no need for anything in writing, except in certain cases such as the sale of land, although, if the matter is at all complex, it is wise to have it in writing to avoid the risk of a dispute about the details of what was agreed.

A contract may be a complex document many pages long, with clauses covering everything from deadline dates to what is to happen if fossils or antiquities are discovered during excavations. (The contract binding me to write this chapter was nine pages long.) On the other hand, a contract may be a simple word-of-mouth agreement: 'That doughnut, please.' 'That will be 35p.' That is a contract, and if I pay with a counterfeit coin or if the doughnut proves unfit to eat, that is a breach of contract. There need not even be words spoken. When I stop my car at the petrol pump I am offering to buy, and by switching on the pump the garage accepts my offer at the price shown on the pump.

Often there will be counter-offers. 'I'll sell you this furniture for £1,000.' 'That's too dear: I'll only give you £800 for it.' 'Not enough: but you can have it for £900.' 'I'll give you £850.' 'OK.' There we have an offer followed by three counter-offers, and the last one is accepted, so there is a legally binding contract at £850.

But a counter-offer 'kills' the previous offer. 'I'll sell you this furniture for £1,000.' 'I'll only give you £800 for it.' 'That's an insult, so I won't sell it to you at all.' 'I didn't mean to upset you! I'll accept your original offer and take the furniture at £1,000.' That is not an acceptance, for the original offer was cancelled by the £800 counter-offer. What the above conversation amounts to is a counter-offer *by the prospective purchaser*, to buy at £1,000, which the owner of the furniture may now accept or refuse. This was laid down as long ago as 1840, in the precedent case of *Hyde* v *Wrench* (1840).[3] This case now forms a 'binding precedent' still valid today.

An acceptance must not impose new conditions. So, if I offer to sell you my car for £5,000, the reply, 'Agreed, provided you put new tyres on it', is not an acceptance. It is a counter-offer, which I may or may not accept.

A person making an offer can withdraw it at any time before it is accepted. And when contracts are made through the post, the contract is binding the moment the acceptance is posted, so if a letter of acceptance and a letter of **revocation** cross in the post, the acceptance prevails and so there is a legally binding contract. (For instantaneous communications such as those by fax and teleprinter, there is another rule. In a case known as the *Entores* case [1955][4] which hinged on whether a contract had been made in London or in Amsterdam, it was held that the place where the contract was made was the place where the acceptance, on teleprinter, was *received*.

'I offer you my car for £5,000 and I promise to keep this offer open for you until the end of next week.' But when you come to me with the money next Friday, you find I have already sold the car to someone else. You have no remedy. Though that promise to keep the offer open was an offer that you accepted, it was not in return for anything. Contrast it with this: 'I offer you my car for £5,000 and if you give me £5 now, I promise to keep the offer open for you until the end of next week' (and you hand me a £5 note.) That is binding. In return for £5 I have promised to do a certain thing, and I am in breach of that £5 contract if I do not do it. In the previous example, my promise was in return for *nothing*, and so it is not legally binding, as it was not a contract.

But that is not the end of this point. If I have made you a promise (even if it is in return for nothing) and I know that you have relied on it, it is against the rule of evidence called 'estoppel' for me to go back on it. This situation arose in the *High Trees* case [1947][5] concerning a block of flats called High Trees House in London. Shortly before the war, the landlord company had leased the entire block to a tenant at a certain rent, and the tenant had intended to sublet the individual flats, at a profit. The outbreak of war in 1939 (and the consequent exodus of thousands of people from London) made the flats difficult to let, so the landlord company told the tenant that it would accept a lower rent for the block. This enabled the tenant to sublet the flats at lower rents and still make a profit. But then, after the flats had been sublet and the tenant was bound by the terms he had agreed with the subtenants, the landlord company went into liquidation, and the liquidator asked for the full rent. The Court of Appeal held (ie decided) that although the landlord company's promise to accept a lower rent had been in return for nothing, it knew that the tenant had committed himself in reliance on that promise, so the court would not hear evidence that the promise did not count and so the promise was binding.

In commercial transactions (goods for sale in a shop, goods advertised in a newspaper, cars in a motor showroom and such like) it is always the customer who makes the offer, which means such goods in your local supermarket are *not* an offer. The customer offers to buy, and the cashier (on behalf of the company) accepts, or could refuse. In *Partridge* v *Crittenden* [1968][6] a man who caught wild birds and advertised them for sale in a magazine was prosecuted for the criminal offence of offering wild birds for sale, but the court had to find him 'not guilty' because a magazine advertisement is not an offer. It is an 'invitation to treat', inviting readers of the advertisement to offer to buy.

Implied terms, exclusion clauses and misrepresentation

The court will imply terms into a contract where this is necessary for 'business efficacy'. Thus, if someone contracts to buy a brand-new machine, there is an implied term that the machine will work. Today this would also be implied under the Sale of Goods Act 1979, by which there is an implied term that goods sold in the course of a business must be of a merchantable quality. But if there is a written contract, beware of the small print. In *L'Estrange* v *Graucob* [1934][7] a shopkeeper bought a cigarette-vending machine. The small print in the contract (which she did not read) contained an 'exclusion clause' saying, 'Any express or implied condition, statement or warranty, statutory or otherwise, is hereby excluded'. The machine did not work and could not be made to work. Such a contract would normally include an implied term that the machine would work, but by signing the contract containing the exclusion clause she had excluded that implication, and so she had no remedy.

If I sell you my computer, that is not in the course of business (as I am not an electrical dealer) so I am not necessarily implying anything about the condition of the computer. I may be selling it 'as seen'. But if you ask me whether the computer is in good mechanical condition, and I reply 'Yes' when the truth is 'No', that is 'misrepresentation' and you have a remedy against me (unless I have persuaded you to sign a written contract with a clause like the one in *L'Estrange* v *Graucob*). But silence is not misrepresentation so, if the buyer does not ask about defects, the seller does not have to mention them.

In *Photo Production Ltd* v *Securicor Transport Ltd* [1980][8] – a House of Lords case about an exclusion clause – the night-watchman sent by Securicor to protect the Photo Production factory negligently started a fire (while playing a game with lighted matches) which caused more than £500,000 damage to the factory. But Securicor's contract with Photo Production Ltd contained a clause that Securicor was not to be liable for any unforeseeable act of its employees, and as this was unforeseeable (as the watchman had never done anything like this before) Securicor did not have to pay for the damage done by its employee.

Under the Unfair Contract Terms Act 1977, there cannot be an exclusion clause whereby a party to the contract can escape liability for causing death or personal injury, but other exclusion clauses are permitted so far as the court sees them as reasonable. There is no remedy in English law for making a bad bargain.

Whether we are dealing with a contract to buy a bun, or a multi-million pound contract 50 pages long, these are the basic rules that apply. In a property context whether the contract is for the carrying out of repairs, maintenance (planned or emergency) or alterations, or a newbuild development, or for letting the property to a tenant, these are still the basic rules.

Tort

A contract is an agreement; a tort is not. A 'tort' is a civil wrong, such as the clumsy reversing of my car by which I put a dent in your car. Nobody agrees to that sort of thing. The most important of the torts is the 'tort of negligence'.

To win a claim for negligence, you must prove three things: (1) the person sued had a duty to be careful; (2) that person was not careful enough; (3) you or your property got damaged as a result. But how far does the duty to be careful extend? Suppose you switch on your new computer and it gives you a severe electric shock, but you had not bought the computer – a friend bought it for you as a gift. Do the manufacturers have a duty to you, or only to your friend?

This point arose in the case of *Donoghue* v *Stevenson* [1932].[9] A man bought a bottle of ginger beer, his girlfriend drank it and was taken ill after finding a rotten snail in it. Is she entitled to compensation? This question is not answered in any Act of Parliament, but the House of Lords judges who heard this case laid down a general principle that if some damage is 'foreseeable as reasonably likely' you must guard against it. With bad ginger beer, it is foreseeable as reasonably likely that whoever drinks it (and not just whoever buys it) will be hurt, so she won compensation.

The important thing to remember (more important than the name or the snail) is this 'foreseeability' principle laid down by the judges. It is a general principle which applies to food, buildings, driving, kicking a ball and all other aspects of life. So, if you are injured by faulty wiring on your friend's new computer, this is the precedent you need to quote, because the manufacturer should have foreseen that it was reasonably likely that anyone at all using the computer would get a shock from it.

During the preparation of this chapter, it was suggested that a precedent case based on faulty building work would be more appropriate than a case about a snail. The answer to that suggestion had to be a firm 'No'. There have been many such cases – for instance *Murphy* v *Brentwood District Council* [1991][10] in which a house was built on a concrete raft which cracked – but a major part of what was being argued in all such cases was whether what happened was foreseeable. And the case that originally laid down the rule, stating that this is what has to be considered, was about a snail in a bottle. That is the case the legal argument will always go back to. That is the way the law works.

The case of *Bourhill* v *Young* [1943][11] went the other way. A motorcyclist, riding negligently, crashed. A pregnant woman getting off a tram, out of sight of the accident, heard the crash and later saw blood on the road as she walked past, and the shock of this caused her to have a miscarriage. The House of Lords held (ie decided) that she was not entitled to any compensation because the motorcyclist could not possibly have foreseen that he would cause this damage to such a person. So here is another general principle: you are not responsible for totally unforeseeable results of your actions.

In *McLoughlin* v *O'Brian* [1982][12] a mother was told that her family had had a car accident. She rushed to the hospital, where she found one of her children dead and the others injured. The shock gave her mental illness, for which she sued the driver of the other car, whose negligence had caused the accident. The House of Lords held that a driver who injures children can foresee that it is reasonably likely that this will give an immense shock to their mother, even if she is not present at the accident.

So, if a child falls down a lift-shaft due to a faulty door in a building for which you are responsible, and as a direct result of this the child's mother suffers a mental breakdown, she can claim compensation for mental illness on the basis of the negligence of your firm, following the precedent of *McLoughlin* v *O'Brian*.

If she had developed mental illness through seeing injury to her neighbour's children, instead of her own children, she would not have received compensation, for there has to be a relationship involving 'close ties of love and affection'. This was laid down by the House of Lords in *Alcock* v *Chief Constable of South Yorkshire Police* [1992][13] (the Hillsborough football disaster case) and this precedent case was followed in *Frost* v *Chief Constable of South Yorkshire Police* [1998][14] in which the House of Lords refused compensation to police officers who suffered mental trauma as rescuers at that disaster. (But if the officers had been physically injured while rescuing victims, they would probably have received compensation.) In this way, the answer to the question, 'How far does a duty to take care extend?' has been developed, and is still being developed, by the courts.

Tort of trespass

Trespass is usually deliberate, whereas negligence is not. It is the difference between deliberately and accidentally putting a dent in your car. If I intentionally kick your car, that is trespass to your goods. If you then kick *me*, that is tort of trespass to my person (as well as being a crime). And if, when my car has failed its MOT test, I dump it on your land, that is trespass to your land. There are many other torts, but the two you are most likely to come across are:

- 'private nuisance', which is something which upsets someone's ordinary use of their land;
- 'public nuisance', which covers such matters as obstructing the highway.

There are also important statutory requirements directly or indirectly connected with Tort, under such Acts as the Occupiers Liability Acts 1957 and 1984, and the Health and Safety at Work Act 1974. Under ss 78E and 78F of the Environmental Protection Act 1990, there are requirements for cleaning up contaminated land and under s 79 of the same statute, certain matters are declared to be a 'statutory nuisance' in respect of which both civil and criminal proceedings may be taken.

Land law

No one owns land in England and Wales. William the Conqueror declared in 1066 that all land was to be held from the Crown and this is still the law today. Today, there are two ways that land can be held: freehold and leasehold. Normally, freehold is held directly and leasehold indirectly from the Crown.

Freehold is a holding directly from the Crown and is for an indefinite period which for practical purposes is perpetual. Its full name is 'fee simple absolute in possession', but this is often shortened to 'fee simple'. ('Fee' is an old English word meaning 'inheritable'.) There are millions of properties held in fee simple. The house in which I and my wife live is a typical example.

On very rare occasions, one might encounter a fee simple held indirectly from the Crown, eg held from the Prince of Wales who holds from the Crown. These are very ancient as the power to make such sub-grants in fee simple was abolished in the year 1290. But it was not abolished for Scotland, which was then a separate kingdom and this is one of the main reasons why Scottish land law is very different from the land law of England and Wales today.

Leasehold is a holding from a landlord. If the lease (or tenancy) is a headlease, the landlord is holding in fee simple from the Crown. If it is a sublease, the landlord is holding from one or more superior landlords, and the head landlord is holding in fee simple from the Crown. Leasehold is for a definite or definable length of time. There are two main types: the leasehold may be for a definite specific length of time such as seven years (this is known as a 'specific term of years absolute') or it may be a recurring period with a definable end, such as a monthly tenancy, recurring at a monthly rent until either the landlord or the tenant defines the end by giving a month's notice to terminate the arrangement. (This is called a 'periodic term of years absolute' – which is a misleading name, as the basic period in this example is not a year but a month.)

Imagine a typical example of commercial leaseholds such as a tall office block. The freehold belongs to the trustees of a pension fund, and they have let the block to your firm on a 99-year lease (that is a specific term of years). Your firm has sublet one floor of the block to a firm, ABC Ltd, for 21 years – another specific term of years.

After five years, ABC Ltd moves out, and sells the residue (ie the remaining 16 years of their lease) to DEF Ltd. This is an 'assignment' of the sublease. DEF Ltd is currently not using the premises but has sub-sublet them on a monthly tenancy (a periodic term of years) to GH Ltd. GH Ltd pays rent to DEF Ltd which pays rent to your firm which pays rent to the trustees of the pension fund.

An 'assignment' means parting with the whole of the leasehold term. A 'subletting' is always for a shorter period than your own term, so that the property will come back to you at the end of the sublease. Thus, in the above example, DEF Ltd will get the property back, one day, and so will your firm. But ABC Ltd will never get it back: they have gone, and DEF Ltd is your firm's tenant in their place.

Typical leasehold properties include most flats (from luxury apartments to student bedsits) and many high street shops, industrial units, houses in many parts of England and Wales, and many other properties. In most leases, there is a clause that the tenant will not assign or sublet without the consent of the landlord.

Do not imagine that it is always easy to get rid of an unwanted tenant. Statutes such as the Landlord and Tenant Acts and the Housing Acts provide a complex web of protections for tenants, ranging from irremovability (in some circumstances) to compensation, with strict rules about the form and timing of notices to quit. If services (gas, electricity, water, sewage) for a property cross other property, 'easements' are required. An easement is a right to do something over other property.

Equity

More than seven hundred years ago it was realised that the 'common law' (the ordinary law, common to everyone) was inadequate in some ways and the King's Chancellor (who was a man of the church) developed a second legal system based on fairness. This second system is 'equity'. There are still two legal systems – common law and equity – today, though since 1875 both of them have been administered by the same courts. In contract, common law will give compensation for breach of contract, but equity will in certain circumstances provide an order for 'specific performance', compelling the unwilling party to complete the contractual obligation. In tort, common law gives compensation, but equity will sometimes provide an order (called a 'prohibitory injunction') to prevent any repetition of the tort – eg 'You will not trespass on that land again'. Breach of an injunction is a contempt of court and will usually result in imprisonment. But it is in land law that equity is most important.

Equity in land law

There is a general rule of thumb in land law that common law says who has to sign the documents for a sale of a property, whereas equity says who gets the money resulting from the sale. In very many cases, a property will be held by 'trustees' on behalf of 'beneficiaries'. The trustees have the legal rights (the common-law rights) but the beneficiaries have the equitable rights.

Sometimes the beneficiaries may be very young, or they may be abroad, or there may be a large number of them. But if a need to sell the property arises, this presents no problem. The trustees sign the documents to sell it, and the trustees are then put under a duty to hand over the proceeds of sale to the beneficiaries at the appropriate time, eg when the beneficiaries reach 18 years of age. So common law makes it easy to sell the property without any delay and equity makes the final result fair, even if it takes a number of years to achieve this goal.

'Co-ownership' always requires trustees. Typical co-ownerships are the freehold or leasehold of a bowling green held by trustees on behalf of all the members of the bowling club, the freehold or leasehold of office premises held by business partners (or, in the case of a large firm, by four partners holding as trustees for all the partners – for there are never more than four trustees) and the freehold or leasehold of a family home held by a husband and wife. In the last-mentioned situation, it is possible (and quite usual) for the husband and wife to appoint *themselves* to be the trustees.

There are two types of co-ownership: joint tenancy and tenancy in common. (The word 'tenancy' is used because, even if the property is freehold, we are all tenants of the Crown.) Joint tenants have an automatic right of survivorship, and this is generally what is wanted by married couples, who desire that if one of them dies, the other of them should be entitled to the whole house. (The right of survivorship overrides anything to the contrary written in a will.) Tenancy in common has no right of survivorship, and is likely to be preferred by business partners, because, when partners die, they are more likely to want their stake in the freehold or leasehold of the firm's premises to go to their families rather than to their business partners.

To be recognised by common law, all leases for a basic period exceeding three years must be written in a legal deed. Shorter leases can be made orally, but this is not recommended as it leads to disputes over precisely what was agreed. All legal leases for longer than 21 years, and all transfers of such leases, and all transfers of legal freeholds, need to be made by deed *and* registered at the Land Registry. If they are made by a written contract, but no deed has been drawn up, they may in certain circumstances be held valid through equity, but registration is still essential, except where the tenant receiving the rights is already in actual occupation of the premises.

An easement made by deed and registered at the Land Registry is a legal easement. If the easement is in writing but is *not* made by a deed, and/or is not registered, it may be recognised as valid by the rules of equity, even though the common law requirements (a deed plus registration) have not been complied with.

Other laws

This chapter has barely brushed the surface. Nothing has been said of planning law – but, for almost every development, planning permission (as to the design and layout of what is to be built) is required, together with Building Regulations consent (as to the standard of materials and workmanship). There are powers to order the demolition of a development not conforming with these requirements.

And then there is tax law, copyright law, employment law and many other types of law. Three series of publications which are of great assistance to anyone seeking to look up the law are *Halsbury's Statutes* (giving the text of nearly all current Acts of Parliament, with extensive footnotes), *Halsbury's Laws of England* (containing a summary of all branches of English law) and *Halsbury's Statutory Instruments* (giving the text of such matters as the Building Regulations). These are available in most large reference libraries. Each series consists of about fifty volumes, well indexed; and they are frequently updated. Annual supplements and loose-leaf additional supplements are provided, and these should always be referred to as the information in the main volumes can very quickly become out of date.

Notes

Abbreviations used in the notes below are as follows:

AC	Law Reports (House of Lords Appeal Cases)
All ER	All England Law Reports
App Cas	Law Reports (Appeal Cases)
Beav.	Beavan's Reports
CA	Court of Appeal
DC	Divisional Court
ER	English Reports
HL	House of Lords
KB	Law Reports (King's Bench Division)
QB	Law Reports (Queen's Bench Division)
TLR	Times Law Reports
WLR	Weekly Law Reports

1   (1878) 3 App Cas 459, HL.
2   (1897) 14 TLR 98, CA.
3   (1840) 3 Beav. 334, 49 ER 132 (a decision of the old Court of Chancery which was replaced by the High Court and Court of Appeal in 1875).
4   *Entores Ltd* v *Miles Far East Corpn*. [1955] 2 QB 327; [1955] 2 All ER 493, CA.
5   *Central London Property Trust Ltd* v *High Trees House Ltd* [1947] KB 130 (a High Court decision by Denning J, later Lord Denning).
6   [1968] 2 All ER 421; [1968] 1 WLR 1204, DC.
7   [1934] 2 KB 394, DC.
8   [1980] AC 827; [1980] 1 All ER 556, HL; [1980] 2 WLR 283.
9   [1932] AC 562, HL.
10 [1991] 1 AC 398; [1990] 2 All ER 908, HL.
11 [1943] AC 92; [1942] 2 All ER 396, HL.
12 [1983] 1 AC 410; [1982] 2 All ER 298, HL.
13 [1992] 1 AC 310; [1991] 4 All ER 907, HL.
14 [1999] 1 All ER 1, HL; [1998] 3 WLR 1509.

Chapter 3

Energy Efficient Buildings

This chapter will provide a background to energy efficient buildings – both their design and use – for the non-professional. Those with professional expertise in building engineering will find it to be a revision of basic principles and it is designed to provide a foundation and framework for the non-expert which will help them to understand technical information.

Those approaching the management of buildings from a non-professional background will find that they may need the advice of a Building Surveyor or Building Services Engineer for solving more complex problems. This chapter will help you understand and implement their advice quickly and efficiently and so save time and money. It will also lessen your reliance on external expertise by showing how energy costs can be reduced by simple, practical measures that can be implemented by the non-professional.

In order to understand how energy costs can be reduced it is necessary to understand how buildings work in terms of their energy consumption and how energy efficiency is measured. Substantial savings can be made simply by targeting those areas which consume the most energy and by giving them first priority in any energy-saving exercise that is carried out. Although there is naturally a wide variation many businesses find that energy efficiency measures are extremely cost effective and have a very short **payback** period.

Most savings on energy expenditure can be achieved by modifying current practice rather than by radical innovations, and in most workplaces there is considerable scope for doing so. The most common reasons that many businesses are not as energy efficient as they could be are listed below.

- It is no one's specific job to manage it.
- There is little understanding of the technical issues involved.
- No one has carried out an energy audit (usually because of the previous two reasons).
- Many firms are trying to solve the wrong problem – overall energy consumption in the workplace can be different from the

domestic energy consumption patterns that most people are familiar with.

- Over-reliance on active rather than passive systems.
- Managers are uncertain how to measure the long term cost effectiveness of energy savings. It is therefore difficult to demonstrate their worth.
- Many firms take a short-term view of investment in energy saving, due to the previous reason.
- Employees have no particular incentive to take the trouble to save someone else's money.
- Equipment is often run inefficiently (due to the previous reason).
- The design of buildings is not always energy efficient.

Of all of these points it is only the last which can be blamed on someone outside the organisation. The other nine can be altered and managed, and as firms often relocate or refurbish their existing facilities then the energy-conscious manager can even have an impact on building design. An understanding of how buildings are designed and how they work is necessary in order to understand how buildings use (and often waste) energy. In the USA points eight and nine have been successfully addressed in many companies by giving a fixed percentage of any money saved to charity. Best results are obtained when the charity is selected by the employees.

The first steps toward energy efficiency can be put into a short checklist as below.

- Appoint a manager or team who is/are specifically responsible for energy efficiency.
- Make sure they know the basics of energy management and how buildings work.
- Carry out an energy audit to identify the main areas for improvement.
- Ensure the improvements can be clearly demonstrated to have a bottom line in terms of cutting costs and can be shown to be cost-effective.

Demonstrating that an idea to save energy is cost-effective is central to the whole field of energy efficiency, and some knowledge of the mathematics involved is necessary to remove the guesswork and uncertainty that can often lead to poor decision making.

Consequently this chapter considers three main aspects to the problem. First we will look at the basic patterns of energy use in

Table 3.1 Energy conversion factors

Fuel	Unit	GJ
Electricity	1 kWh	0.0036
Gas	1 therm	0.105
Fuel oil	1 litre	0.042
Coal (average quality)	1 tonne	28.00

buildings and then at how an **energy audit** can best be undertaken. Finally we will consider the mathematics involved.

Buildings and energy use

Most businesses consume gas and electricity exactly as most homes do. Electricity is measured in kilowatt hours, usually amended to kWh on your bill. An electrical device rated at 2 kilowatts per hour and switched on for 100 hours per month will therefore use 200 kilowatt hours. Gas is measured in British thermal units, usually abbreviated to either BTU or therms on your bill, although some gas suppliers convert the amount to its electrical 'equivalent' and show kilowatt hours on their invoice. The 'common denominator' of all types of energy is the gigajoule, and if your facility uses more than one type of energy it is a good idea to see if you are spending money on a type of fuel that gives you less gigajoules per pound than the alternative. Table 3.1 shows how different kinds of energy measure up against each other.

As you see one therm of gas will deliver the same amount of energy as 30 kWh of electricity, and you should clearly be aware of such considerations when assessing your fuel bill. Those fuel types with the highest cost per gigajoule and which make up the largest percentage of the facility's energy budget should be prioritised, although you should remember that conversion from one fuel type to another can be very expensive and may outweigh any short- or medium-term savings.

What type of fuel your facility uses, and how that use is structured can vary enormously, depending on what kind of business we are discussing. However, there are common patterns within businesses of the same type and a reliable set of averages can be found in Table 3.2.

Table 3.2 Percentage of energy costs by building type

	Office	Ware-house*	Retail	Factory**	Domestic	Hotel
Heat	55	80+	55	70	55	50
Light	20	10	25	20	10	10
Air conditioning	10		10			
Hot water	10	2	5	5	20	15
Cooking					10	15
Other	5	8	5	5	5	10

* In a refrigerated warehouse the cost for cooling is also 80+ per cent.

** This excludes production machinery as there is too much variety to set a reliable average.

The two main targets for energy efficiency can be identified at once – heat and light. These costs often make up at least 70 per cent of energy expenditure, and as time is always at a premium they should be prioritised in any energy-efficiency programme.

The Building Regulations

There are minimum standards of energy efficiency which a building must conform to by law, and these are specified in Section L of the Building Regulations. The Regulations as we know them today evolved from the Public Health Acts introduced in the nineteenth century to stop developers putting up cheap, unhygenic and shoddy buildings. They are in effect quality control regulations for building designers and construction companies.

Section L specifies the highest legal **U-values** a building can incorporate. A U-value is simply a number that specifies how thermally efficient an element of a building (such as a wall) can be. Calculating U-values is a job for specialists. All you need to know is that the *lower* the U-value the better, hence the specification of legal *maximums* in the Regulations. The Regulations themselves are updated every few years, and the government almost invariably makes U-values tighter (lower) in each instance. Such 'upgrades' only apply to buildings subsequent to that date and do not oblige the owners of existing buildings to improve their energy efficiency.

The Regulations are flexible, so allowing designers and builders freedom of choice within a set of overall constraints. This means there are three methods of assessment (if we do not count domestic buildings): the elemental method, the calculation method and the energy use method.

The elemental method is the simplest and the oldest method of assessment and simply specifies that for each part (element) of a building the U-value shall not be higher than that specified in the Regulations above. The calculation method allows designers to trade off good and bad U-values in their building and so frees them from rigid constraints. Higher than average U-values in some elements (eg windows) can be allowed as long as lower than average U-values are achieved in other elements, so compensating to average out at a level equal to the elemental method. The energy use method allows designers to make use of **solar gain** and other innovative approaches to energy efficiency. It necessitates a complex measurement of a building's energy efficiency by building professionals, who must use an official **Standard Assessment**

Procedure or SAP. The building is then given an SAP rating. There is some degree of overlap in these methods; the elemental U-values given above apply to buildings with an SAP rating of 60 or over. Buildings with an SAP rating of *under 60* (more energy efficient) are permitted marginally lower elemental U-values.

If you are dealing with older buildings, it is certain they will have been designed to higher (less stringent) U-values, as shown below (only walls are shown in order to give an overall idea of recent changes):

Year	U-value for exposed walls
1965	1.47
1976	0.6
1986	0.35
1995	0.25

The long-term pattern is for substantial improvements in the thermal efficiency of buildings.

Building costs: construction versus operational

Generally speaking, there are two types of costs for buildings: the cost of construction and the costs of operation. Over a building's lifetime, it is possible for the former to be less than the latter. Certainly operational costs can be extremely high and energy can be among the most significant item of expenditure. Until recently most firms tended to emphasise construction costs at the expense of operational costs, but as businesses become more aware of the amount of money they spend on energy, maintenance and running costs, they are beginning to see that cutting back on construction costs can be a false economy in the long term.

A classic example of this was the public housing tower blocks of the 1950s and 1960s. Construction costs were cut to the bone and the result was a building that was cheap to construct but which was poorly insulated and needed a high level of maintenance expenditure due to the use of low-quality construction materials. The lifts were the cheapest on the market and so were always breaking down and many residents could not afford to turn the heat on as the contractors had only concerned themselves with which heating system was the cheapest to install, not the cheapest to run.

Now businesses pay much more attention to the **life cycle cost** of systems and use numerical methods to find out which building or component represents the best value for money over the long term. To give a simple example – is it worth installing double glazing into a new office building at a cost of £40,000 if it will save £3,000 per year in heating costs over the next twenty years and the current interest rate (for borrowing the money to do so) is 5 per cent? Such questions can be crucial to the field of energy management and an understanding of life cycle costing, along with **net savings** methodologies, is necessary in all but the very smallest premises. Only by using such methods is it possible to demonstrate that a proposed energy scheme is cost-effective (or not) and so make a clear case for investment in energy efficiency. One of the simplest ways to do this is by showing the payback period of an investment. An investment in energy-saving technology that pays for itself in a couple of years is likely to be very popular with senior management and receive priority funding. The payback period for many areas of energy-saving technology is often significantly less than is commonly imagined.

Those firms with a strong 'green' agenda also consider the concept of **embodied energy** in their building design and component specification. This again belongs to the realm of the specialist but guides exist to show you how different systems and components can be graded for their 'green' credentials and overall energy consumption

The government's **fiscal policy** can affect the balance between construction and operational costs in buildings, although currently it is far more likely to rely on **direct policy** such as the Building Regulations. VAT on energy will make it more expensive to use and so will make it more cost-effective to be energy efficient (as intended). So called 'green' taxes already exist in such provisions as the tax on landfill dumping and are aimed at protecting the environment. As these taxes are periodically amended and a range of exemptions exist, it is necessary to keep a keen eye on current policy.

Conducting an energy audit

An energy audit is comparable to a financial audit. It is an attempt to cost, analyse and evaluate expenditure on energy and to identify both problems and opportunities. Large organisations will almost certainly find a professional audit worthwhile, but it is perfectly feasible for medium or small firms to conduct their own

Professional energy audits

This chapter is designed to enable you to be as energy efficient as possible and should help you to make significant savings on your energy costs. However, for large organisations or those with complex plant and equipment, professional help could be worthwhile. If professional expertise is deemed necessary then this guide should help you work closely with the experts and cut down your reliance on them, so saving on fees. It will also enable you to specify exactly what help you need and precisely what information you need from them, which will also save money. Your local Energy Efficiency Office (see Useful Addresses at the end of the book) will be able to put you in contact with a reputable company with experience in any particular area you need.

There are two common types of service provided. The first is a fixed fee contract where the consultants will provide you with a list of advice and recommendations after conducting an energy audit of your facilities. The level of the fee will depend on how large your premises are and how much plant and equipment they use.

The second (and usually the best value) is a savings percentage contract. The consultants will receive an agreed percentage of all the energy expenditure that you save following their energy audit. There is no 'standard' percentage and it is well worth shopping around between consultancies. Whichever firm you do business with obviously has the strongest possible incentive to be detailed, thorough and professional in their advice, and to make sure that the measures they recommend are the most cost-effective possible. Some firms will simply give advice, leaving you to make a separate arrangement with another company to carry it out. Other firms will contract to put into effect all the measures they recommend and this can range from installing thermostats to large-scale overhauls of equipment. The amount of money saved is usually taken from an average of one year's billing before the contract was taken out, in order to make sure that seasonal variations such as higher winter fuel bills do not skew the figure one way or another. The larger and more energy-hungry your premises, the more worthwhile an outsourced contract is, especially as many firms undertake the original audit at their own expense. If they cannot save you any money you pay nothing.

Conducting your own energy audit

The smaller your facility the less cost-effective a professional energy audit will be. Even so it is often well worth conducting your own 'informal' audit and this section is designed to help you do so effectively rather than simply relying on a semi-planned walkabout by management in the hope of finding glaring examples of waste which can be speedily corrected.

Audits should be undertaken after each of the following:

- purchase or lease of new premises;
- alteration in production schedules;
- change of use of the space, such as office reshuffle;
- change in energy supplier;
- introduction of new working practices such as flexitime, new shifts, hot desking;
- extension or refurbishment of premises.

Scale of audit

The scale of an audit can vary substantially. A brief walkabout by management can take a morning or perhaps a whole day, and be concerned with spotting the more glaring examples of waste in the premises and taking steps to cut them out. Such a basic level of auditing will pay high dividends for a small amount of time and effort and is usually called 'housekeeping'. Housekeeping audits tend to use little or no direct measurement of energy flows, but rather rely on commonsense identification of malpractice or neglect. A housekeeping audit can be a useful foundation to build on and can be a cost-effective first step while a more detailed energy audit is being planned and considered.

There is no fixed rule of how detailed an audit should be as every business is unique. The larger the business facilities and the more energy they consume then the more cost-effective an in-depth audit will be.

Before starting an audit, it is advisable to consider the following:

- **How are you going to monitor energy patterns?**
  Usually a chart correlating different areas or different facilities with energy consumption will provide a very useful first step and allow graphs and tables to be produced. Setting out to conduct an energy audit without a predetermined method of recording data will constitute a poor use of time and effort.

- **Where are the meters?**

  No energy audit can be made without them. Building blueprints should reveal their location, and individual members of staff may know of any recently installed meters in their office or workshop. Mark these additions onto your blueprints for further use. The more meters there are the more concise your energy audit can be. One meter for the whole facility allows little analysis of where the main energy drains occur. Meters can be hired from energy consultancies and 'plugged in' to an area or room to measure its individual energy consumption.

- **When should the audit be undertaken?**

  Seasonal variations, especially in heating, can be enormous and you should be aware of this before you start. Calculating the heating bill for July is worse than useless for predicting energy consumption in November. An audit undertaken in December can be compared to one undertaken in April and one in July to provide an overall picture. It may be possible to sidestep this delay simply by looking at last year's bills.

What time of day the audit is conducted can also have an effect on the outcome, especially if shiftwork and flexitime are part of working practice. Try as far as possible to take a typical working day and a typical shift. Undertaking an audit at weekends or during factory shutdown can also be extremely useful. It identifies the precise energy load of plant and machinery that is not being used by comparing consumption patterns to those during normal production schedules.

For an initial energy audit it may be useful to conduct three separate studies, one of the building fabric, one of the services within it and one of building use. This will simplify what is potentially a complex programme and guard against piling up too much data to comfortably digest and analyse.

Building fabric will have a great effect on energy consumption. Newer buildings will be designed to lower U-values and older buildings to higher U-values. Older buildings are more likely to suffer from deterioration of components and so waste energy from draughts and exposure. For larger, older premises it may be worth hiring a thermal image camera which can show up substantial cold spots which indicate where heat is being wasted as a result of deteriorated insulation.

Building fabric

The three main areas of the building's fabric that need to be checked are walls, windows and roofs as these are the most common areas of heat loss. The addition of insulation and draught proofing can be very cost effective. Walls with poor insulation standards can be improved by the addition of foam cavity wall insulation, and those with single skin sheeting such as corrugated metal (usually in factory spaces) can have their thermal efficiency substantially improved by the addition of insulation board on the inside. Roof spaces provide perhaps the easiest and most cost effective scope for retrofitted insulation. Windows are another common area of heat loss, although it is very rarely worth removing perfectly serviceable single glazed windows to replace them with double glazing. If the windows are in such a poor state of repair that they need replacing anyway then double glazing could be worthwhile. Even then it is worth checking the relative cost of low energy glazing. By far the most cost effective measure is to draught strip windows and doors and so cut down on heat loss.

Building services

Services can be usefully subdivided into heating, lighting, hot water, and mechanical ventilation. For each of these a simple checklist of questions can be drawn up.

Heating
• Is the boiler working efficiently?
• Are thermostats set to the correct temperature?
• What timing switches exist?
• Are they set correctly?
• Is pipework in the boiler room insulated?
• Is the boiler heated by the most cost-effective fuel source?
• Is a **combined heat and power** system worth installing?
• How much energy is being used?

Hot water
• Are hot water pipes and tanks insulated?
• Are thermostats set correctly in terms of temperature and occupation periods?
• Is hot water being used for industrial purposes where cold water could be?

- Is the volume being stored and heated more than is actually required?
- Are pipe runs from boiler to point of use longer than necessary?
- How much energy is being used?

Mechanical ventilation
- Could natural ventilation be used sometimes?
- Are thermostats and timing controls set correctly?
- Are the ducts leak free, and are filters regularly cleaned?
- Is pumped air provided to areas that do not need it?
- Is the proportion of air recirculated as high as possible?
- Cross-check thermostats with heating system thermostats to ensure both systems are not on at the same time.
- How much energy is being used?

Lighting
- Has energy-efficient lighting been installed? (It usually has a payback period of under three years.)
- Is the lighting provided the right amount for the task (see Table 3.3)?
- Can natural daylight be used instead of artificial light?
- Would the installation of automatic lighting controls be cost-effective?
- It is a common myth that fluorescent lights cost money to switch on and off; if they are not in use, switch them off.
- How much energy is being used?

There are limitations to how much energy can be saved on lighting as Health and Safety regulations specify minimum levels, as shown in Table 3.3.

These are only rough figures for preliminary guidance and if you are in any doubt at all you should consult the health and safety inspector. The level of lux (unit of lighting) can be measured with a meter that can be hired via your local Energy Efficiency Office. The meter should be placed on the work surface being checked. Be wary of trying to economise too greatly on lighting levels – it may lead to complaints and a visit from the health and safety inspector.

Building use

Buildings are often utilised in a different way from that originally intended, especially if they are older. Even with newer buildings innovations such as hot desking, teleworking and the fashion for

Table 3.3 Task lighting: recommended minimums

Task	lux
Corridors, loading bays, storerooms	150
Packing, large-scale assembly	300
General offices, detailed assembly	500
Draughting office, quality control	750
Electronic component/fine assembly	1,000

open-plan office space mean that traditional occupancy patterns are not always still applicable. The audit should check what time personnel arrive, what time they leave and what shifts are worked. This should be correlated to timing switches and thermostats on service control systems. Some work practice innovations such as flexitime and hot desking may mean staff use the buildings at evenings and weekends and this could necessitate alterations to automatic control systems.

It is cost effective to divide the building up into areas or zones which have their own individual control systems for heating and lighting so that heat and light is only provided to those specific areas that need it. This already exists in many workplaces – individual rooms have their own radiator control and light switches.

Open-plan office space can present problems and if only a small number of staff are occupying a large area, it is clearly less energy-efficient than closed-plan space, especially if flexible working practices mean it is in use seven days per week.

Occupancy patterns can provide scope for the use of low-tariff gas and electricity. Most companies charge lower rates for night-time use and this should be considered in industrial premises that work shifts. Measuring energy use over a typical 24-hour period will provide a breakdown of potential savings by identifying patterns of high and low use.

Energy purchasing

Deregulation of the gas and electricity markets means that the energy manager has considerable scope to shop around and compare prices. Coal and oil are different in terms of market structure but there is still scope to compare prices from different suppliers. Past invoices from suppliers provide a ready-made source

Table 3.4 Energy by type and cost

Type	Units purchased	G J	% of total bill
Gas	10,500 therms	1,102.5	25
Electricity	208,000 kWh	748.8	57
Coal	50 tonnes	1,400	18

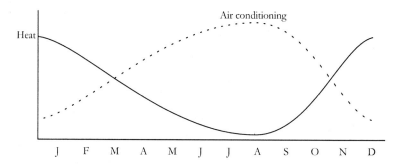

Figure 3.1 Energy consumption over one year

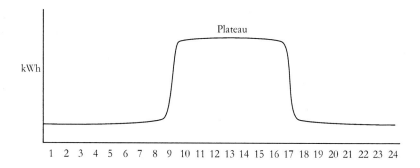

Figure 3.2 Energy consumption over 24 hours

source of data that can be quickly analysed and which should highlight long-term trends in the facility's energy consumption patterns. It may be that fuel consumption has gone up 4 per cent each year for the last three years, and such figures need to be checked against output. If production has gone up 4 per cent for the last three years, there is not necessarily a problem. In considering any purchase the following points should be considered.

Different suppliers may have different levels of competitiveness in different areas, and you should consider what the overall benefit is rather than just considering straightforward unit cost. For electricity there will be a standing charge that is fixed irrespective of level of use. Units (kWh) will be charged at both day tariffs and night tariffs and there may be substantial variations. Weekend use may also qualify for a cheaper rate. There may also be a 'maximum demand' step charge which places a higher charge on units over a certain level. On the other hand, large companies may qualify for discounts. There will be similar variations in gas prices. Again, large companies can negotiate a lower price per therm, but they tend to pay a larger standing charge than smaller companies.

The complex and competitive nature of deregulated supply means that there is no longer a straightforward strategy for minimising energy expenditure. Individual negotiations with a range of different suppliers is the best way to ensure value for money, in much the same way as buying any other commodity.

Whatever fuel you use metering is the key to any energy strategy. In a large facility with a small number of meters it may well be worth paying for more to be installed. The more specific you can be about where and when energy is being used, the more efficient you can be in cutting down on its use.

Presenting your data

Now that all your data has been processed you can present it in various kinds of charts and tables that can be cross-referenced and cross-correlated. Table 3.4 and Figures 3.1 and 3.2 are examples of common and concise ways of presenting data.

Mathematical methods for assessing energy efficiency

Few people take naturally to mathematics, but it is essential to be able to show clear, concise calculations of the cost-effectiveness of energy efficiency schemes. The alternative is quite simple: you must *guess* if a particular energy-saving scheme is going to save or lose you money. The problem with many energy efficiency proposals is the fact that they often cost money to implement *now* whereas the money they save will take a few years to add up to a 'profit'. How much money is saved and how long it takes to cover the costs are crucial questions, and mathematical tools such as life cycle costing and net savings can provide the answers.

Life cycle costing can be extremely complex when undertaken at its most sophisticated level, but there is considerable scope for its use at a more down-to-earth level and it is vital to understand its use and methods. By giving firm statistical data on the cost-effectiveness of energy-efficiency measures, it brings them out of the realm of vague speculation and allows clear-cut judgments to be made on what is and what is not cost-effective. As with many mathematical methods it looks complex to begin with, but can readily be understood with a little practice.

What life cycle costing does is to take into account *both* the construction (or installation) costs of a building or building component *and* its operational costs over its lifetime, and add them together so that different systems can be compared and the most cost-effective selected. Similar systems (such as lights) have both different installation costs and different operational costs. Energy efficient lamps cost far more to install than conventional lamps but are far cheaper to run. Using life cycle cost techniques allows us to compare the financial benefits of each. It is therefore a 'cradle to grave' approach, and considers purchase cost, installation cost, running cost and maintenance cost. It can even take into account the disposal costs of a system, such as the costs of safely disposing of chlorofluorocarbon (CFC) gases used in air-conditioning systems.

There are two principal life cycle costing techniques, the **present value** method and the **annual value** method. The annual value method has the advantage of being able to compare the cost effectiveness of systems that have very different lifespans, but is much more complex. Consequently, we shall look at how the present value method is used. It only compares systems that have similar lifespans, but is easier for the beginner to learn. After you become familiar with it you can use it as a basis to develop your understanding of the annual value method if necessary. The present value method converts all current and future costs to today's terms, and expresses them as a *lump sum* at current prices.

Explaining the method and its use

There are many textbooks that will provide you with the mathematical tools necessary to conduct quite complex life cycle cost studies, and in order to do so will provide you with mathematical formulae that – while by no means inaccessible – are perhaps left to more advanced study. Here we will try and 'sidestep' the formulae, and as we will be looking at straight-forward examples this can be done without sacrificing accuracy.

We will use Tables B and C given in Appendix 1 at the end of the text as the basis for calculations. These allow us to convert all the money spent (or saved) in the future into the equivalent of a single lump sum at *today's prices*. When using the tables you should bear in mind that the year a project is initiated is always taken to be year zero. The following year is counted as year one, and so forth.

It is necessary to convert future costs (and savings) to present value pounds (in other words to today's prices), so that different systems can be compared to each other on a *common* basis.

Because of inflation, £1,000 spent (or received) this year is worth more than £1,000 spent or received next year, and the further we go into the future the less it is worth. Consequently it is customary to use tables to convert all future sums of money into what they would be worth today, so allowing a fair comparison to be made. This is necessary because different systems have different patterns of costs over their lifespans. If we take two air-conditioning systems each with a lifespan of 20 years, we may find that system A costs £80,000 to install and has annual running and maintenance costs of £8,000 whereas system B costs £73,000 but has annual running and maintenance costs of £9,000. Is the £7,000 saved on installation costs this year worth £1,000 per year for the next ten years or not? The question becomes more complex when we have to account for the cost of borrowing the money for the installation costs – interest has to be paid each year on £80,000 for system A, but only on £73,000 for system B. To account for these variations, we set a **discount rate**.

The discount rate

This enables us to take into account both inflation and interest rates and gives us a number which we use to convert all future costs (and savings) to present value terms by looking that number up in Table B or C in Appendix 1.

It may be argued initially that a firm does not have to borrow money to finance a project but could instead use its own funds, and that therefore it is wrong to take into account interest payments. This ignores the **opportunity cost** of capital. If a firm installs an air conditioning system at a cost of £80,000 from its own funds then it is losing the interest it could have received from simply keeping the £80,000 in the bank. Taking the money out and spending it could be losing the company £5,000 per year in interest payments. So even if the money is taken from the firm's own capital we still need to take into account the interest rate. The discount rate is often expressed as a decimal fraction in the full formula, so 7 per cent becomes 0.07. Some firms refer to the discount rate as the 'cost of capital'.

The study period

It is important to establish a time frame for any life cycle cost project. How long into the future are we going to look?

The time frame chosen is usually referred to as the study period. There is a danger of this being arbitrary due to the fact that there is no clear-cut time scale for some energy efficiency measures. Double glazing once installed will probably last as long as the building, whereas other systems, such as air-conditioning systems, have a relatively limited lifespan, after which they will need either replacing or a substantial overhaul. Even this can be hard to predict with certainty; an air-conditioning system that is expected to last around 25 years can have a useful life of five years either way. For this reason analysts often like to conduct a **sensitivity analysis** which will be examined later in this chapter.

Despite the fact that there is rarely an absolute definition of what study period is most appropriate it nonetheless allows us to take a view of events over a fixed horizon, rather than to try and make calculations with no time scale in mind. Firms often use study periods of 10, 15 or 20 years as straightforward time scales with which to analyse projects. It means several rival systems such as heating installations can be compared and the one with the lowest life cycle cost selected. It may not have the lowest *installation* cost, but the formula ensures that it will have the lowest *overall* cost over the 20 years it is in use.

Costs over time

It is vital that the year a cost occurs can be identified as the nearer it is to the present then the greater a weighting it is afforded. The further into the future a cost occurs, the lower a weighting it is afforded. The extreme position of this is the year a system is to be installed. These costs do not need to be adjusted as they are already measured in present value pounds – today's prices. The tables presented at the back of this book help in calculating what weighting should be given to a future cash flow. Tables A, B and C have all been set at two decimal places for the sake of simplicity. Some texts take them to four or five decimal places, but such precision is only needed by mathematicians and professional building economists who need to be absolutely accurate as they are often dealing with tens of millions of pounds. Table A is not always needed in such calculations, but is included for reference as it shows how much a given amount of money will earn (or cost) at a given rate of interest over a given time, and can be used to calculate the impact of inflation. You should note that it is standard practice to use the letter t in such tables to refer to a particular year. The current year is always expressed as $t = 0$. Next year would be $t = 1$ and so on.

Using the tables

For those not used to manipulating formulae Tables B and C given in Appendix 1 exist to summarise the effects of discounting. These are very handy 'ready reckoners' and save having to make the series of long-hand calculations implicit in the formula. Table B shows the present value of 'one-off ' future cash flows and allows us to convert them to present value terms straightaway. For instance, if we were using a discount rate of 3 per cent and wanted to convert the cost of a £7,000 overhaul taking place ten years from now we would look up 3 per cent at ten years and find the factor to be 0.74. When multiplied by 7,000 the result is 5,180. This means £7,000 spent in ten years time is the equivalent of £5,180 spent today when we take into account both inflation and interest rates.

Table C does the same for *annually recurring* costs such as fuel consumption. If a heating system cost £2,000 per year to run and we wanted to know what this would come to over 15 years at 3 per cent we would look in Table C and find the factor to be 11.94. When multiplied by 2,000 the result is 23,880. This means that £2,000 spent each year for 15 years is the equivalent of £23,800 in today's terms when we take into account inflation and interest rates.

Learning to use the tables in this way does not take very long, and is far quicker than going through the formula step by step which can be cumbersome and time-consuming.

Although using these tables will allow you to 'sidestep' the formula you should still take the time to understand the principles on which it operates so that you understand what you are doing.

Calculating life cycle costs

Using mathematical methods can be difficult to begin with and two examples are included to help clarify the process. The first example involves the life cycle costing of an energy efficient lighting system and making a comparison to the **baseline alternative** of a conventional system. The second example looks at the net savings technique and shows how to calculate which of two air-conditioning systems is the most cost-effective.

Example 1

An import/export company is considering the installation of energy efficient lighting into four of their warehouses in an effort to cut down on energy costs and want to know if it is cost-effective or not.

The current annual running costs for lighting is £2,000 including maintenance, repairs and energy costs.

Purchase and installation of an energy efficient system will cost £3,200 and annual running costs are estimated to be £800. The company has specified a ten-year study period and a discount of 4 per cent. Is the new system cost effective?

Method

1 Purchase and installation costs are £3,200. This takes place in the current year and so does not need to be adjusted. Running costs occur annually and so do need to be adjusted. From Table C the factor for ten years at 4 per cent is 8.11. When this factor is multiplied by £800 it shows the total running costs to be £6,488 when expressed as a *lump sum at today's prices*.

2 The installation costs plus the running costs over ten years can therefore be shown as:

£3,200
£6,488
—————
£9,688   Total life cycle costs

3 This must now be compared to the baseline alternative of not having the system installed. As the current lighting system is already in operation there are no installation costs. However, there are running and maintenance costs of £2,000. These are multiplied by the same factor of 8.11 in order to work out the cost of £2,000 per year for ten years in today's terms.

4 £2,000 × 8.11 is £16,220
The total cost of the energy saving lighting is therefore £6,532 cheaper than the baseline alternative and is well worth the higher installation costs.

Example 2

Following a recent merger, the IT section of a company is to be moved to a new building. The building does not have any air conditioning and so a new system will need to be installed. There are a range of systems on the market, but eventually the search is narrowed down to two, both having a working life of 20 years.

System A is expensive but has lower running and maintenance costs. To purchase and install it will cost £14,000; annual running and maintenance costs are estimated to be £1,250 and after ten years it will need a complete overhaul, estimated to cost £2,500.

System B is cheaper to buy but more expensive to run and maintain. To purchase and install it will cost £12,500; annual running and maintenance costs are estimated to be £1,750 and after ten years it will need a complete overhaul, estimated to cost £3,500.

The study period is set at 20 years as this is the working life of both systems. If the company specifies a discount rate of 7 per cent which is the most cost-effective?

Method

The net savings of a system are calculated simply by taking the life cycle cost of each and deducting the lower cost from the higher. In this case the systems are not optional but mandatory because the IT facility must be air conditioned. If it were an ordinary office facility with little in the way of IT then air conditioning would be optional. Because it is mandatory there is no baseline alternative.

1 System A costs £14,000 to purchase and install. This takes place in the current year and so does not need to be adjusted.

2 Annual running costs do need adjusting. In Table C the factor for 20 years at 7 per cent is 10.59. So, £1,250 multiplied by 10.59 equals £13,237, which is the total running cost expressed as an annual sum at today's prices.

3 The cost of the overhaul in year ten must also be added to the total, and here we use Table B. The factor for ten years at 7 per cent is 0.51. This means that £2,500 spent in ten years' time is the same £1,275 today, and is arrived at by multiplying £2,500 by 0.51.

4 The total is therefore:

Purchase installation cost	£14,000
Annual running cost	£13,237
Overhaul in year 10	£1,275
Life cycle cost	£28,512

Exactly the same process can now be applied to System B:

1   Installation costs are £12,500
2   Running costs are £1,750 × 10.59 or £18,532.
3   Overhaul costs are £3,500 × 0.51 or £1,785.
4   The total is therefore:

Purchase and installation costs	£12,500
Annual running costs	£18,532
Overhaul in year 10	£1,785
Life cycle cost	£32,817

System A is clearly cheaper over the full 20-year period. The net saving is arrived at simply by deducting the lower cost from the higher and is £4,305.

Sensitivity analysis

Sensitivity analysis is a method for checking how safe a decision is once the life cycle cost or net saving has been calculated. In the real world variables are subject to unpredictable changes. Interest rates may be higher than expected, the maintenance costs of a new heating system may be lower than expected or its energy consumption higher. For this reason, it is highly advisable to conduct a sensitivity analysis once your results have been reached. It is not as complex as it may initially sound. All that is done is to take a given variable – maintenance costs for instance – and see what would happen to the final figure if they turned out to be higher than anticipated. Would the project still be worthwhile?

If it turns out that even a small increase in running costs or a slight change in the discount rate used means that the project is no longer economic then it is a risky proposition. If, on the other hand, it can be shown that even if a system uses more energy than expected or costs more to maintain than anticipated and still saves money then it is a relatively risk-free option. A sensitivity analysis is therefore a way of measuring what margin of error there is in a decision.

For instance, if it turned out that the annual running costs of the new lighting system mentioned in Example 1 were £1,000 instead of £800 would it still be worth installing? As it is only one variable that is being questioned *everything else stays the same*. The £1,000 would be multiplied by 8.11 to show running costs (over ten years) of in present value terms.

This would be added to the existing data as shown below:

Installation costs	£3,200
Running costs	£8,110
Life cycle costs	£11,310

So even if the costs of the new lighting were 25 per cent higher than anticipated, they would still generate a net saving and have a lower life cycle cost than the baseline alternative. Sensitivity analysis exercises can therefore be very useful tools for convincing senior management that a proposition is (or is not) cost-effective. It can be taken further and figures calculated up to the point of where a scheme is no longer cost-effective in order to demonstrate the margin of error in a proposal. For instance, the cost of running the new lighting would have to be over double the original estimate before it would mean their costs outweighed their savings.

You should appreciate that changing the discount rate used and the study period selected can also be part of a sensitivity analysis. Study periods are crucial to the viability of energy-efficiency measures as they can cost a lot of money initially and save smaller amounts of money for many, many years. A short study period will tend to overemphasise costs and underemphasise savings.

You should also be able by now to see how the tables in Appendix 1 work. Why is the £3,500 spent in ten years' time in Example 2 worth £910 at today's prices at a rate of 7 per cent? If we took £910 today and let it accumulate in the bank for ten years what would it be worth? Check Table A for 20 years at 7 per cent. The factor given is 3.87. Multiply this by £910 and see the result (the tiny error is because we have rounded the Tables to two decimal places). Tables B, C and D are all derived from the formula used to calculate Table A.

Setting the discount rate

Setting a discount rate can involve long calculations, but a very good working value can be arrived at simply. All you need to do is find the current interest rate on money your firm borrows and the current inflation rate and deduct one from the other. For instance if the interest rate was 7 per cent and the inflation rate was 4 per cent we would use a discount rate of 3 per cent in our calculations. It may not even be necessary to do this as many large companies have a discount rate already decided upon – often referred to as the 'cost of capital'.

Individual companies may end up using different discount rates because of their different 'time weighting' of money, which can prompt them to add or subtract a couple of percentage points from their calculations. This is because different firms attach different priorities to spending now versus spending in the future. Firms with surplus cash may be quite happy to spend it now. Firms with a cash flow problem attach a greater significance to current spending and would rather spend less money now and more money later.

This means firms can add or subtract percentage points from the derived discount rate to take into account their individual circumstances. If a firm attaches a great significance to current spending and would rather avoid spending money now unless it absolutely has to it will select a higher discount rate. However, unless your firm has a clear policy on this you should use the method shown above.

Once a discount rate has been set it allows future expenditure and future savings to be adjusted to show what they are in present value terms, and so see (for instance) if spending £10,000 this year is worth a saving of £1,000 per year over the next 15 years.

It is particularly important in energy-saving calculations because firms incorrectly make investment decisions that emphasise income generated over expenditure saved. This is because money saved does not appear on company accounts whereas income generated does. Potential savings therefore remain entirely invisible and so are put to one side in favour of less cost-effective projects that generate income. For instance a real estate investment company may choose to spend £50,000 on buying a house which it then leases for £4,000 per year. If the same £50,000 were spent on installing energy efficient heating in its national headquarters, it could save £5,000 per year. The second option is clearly the most sensible, but will not appear in the accounts and so does not get approval. Using a discounting system such as life cycle costing or net savings permits such projects to be assessed.

Sinking funds

No system or component lasts forever and everything will one day need replacing. It is good practice to set aside a small amount of money each year to replace items of capital expenditure rather than be faced with a large bill to be settled all at once. The usual practice is to start a **sinking fund** at a bank so that a regular annual deposit can accumulate interest over 10 or 15 years and so be withdrawn as a lump sum when it is needed.

Calculating how much something will cost in the future is never certain and it is advisable to slightly overestimate in order to provide a margin of error. Table A in Appendix 1 shows the relative value of £1 as it accumulates interest over the years. It can also be used to estimate by how much the cost of something will increase if a given rate of inflation is assumed. For instance, if over the next 15 years inflation is assumed to average 4 per cent, then a factor of 1.8 is used to estimate the (approximate) replacement cost of an item in 15 years' time. If a system of infra-red room lighting controls costs £12,000 to install now and will need replacing in 15 years' time, it can be calculated to cost 1.8 × £12,000 = £21,600 when a new system needs to be installed. This would usually be rounded up to £22,000. Table D would then be used to estimate how much money would need to be set aside each year to provide a lump sum of £22,000 in 15 years' time. A savings account can be opened with a fixed interest rate, and this allows the calculations to be precise. If the interest rate on savings was 7 per cent, then for 15 years a figure of 0.03979 is given in Table D. This is multiplied by £22,000 and gives £875.38. This shows that £875.38 set aside each year at 7 per cent for 15 years will give £22,000 at the end of it. Cautious managers may wish to round the sum up to £880 or even £900. This is because there is no certain way to predict inflation over the long term. Even so, the sinking fund method is a substantial advance on simply guessing how much needs to be set aside.

Payback

Payback is one of the simplest and most direct ways of demonstrating the cost effectiveness of a project. The shorter the payback period the more cost effective a project is. 'Simple payback' does not need any complex calculations in terms of inflation or interest rates and can be worked out in a matter of seconds, as shown below.

$$\text{Payback} = \frac{\text{Investment cost}}{\text{Annual savings}}$$

For instance, if double glazing costs £42,000 to install and saves £7,500 per year on heating bills its payback period would be:

$$\frac{42,000}{7,500} = 5.6 \text{ years}$$

Although payback is very popular due to its relative simplicity there is a price to be paid for using it. It is a very blunt instrument, and because it takes no account of the time value of money (as expressed by the interest rate and inflation) it represents only a very rough-and-ready assessment of a project's profitability. Most seriously it fails to take into account a project's savings *after* the payback period.

In certain circumstances some projects may save very little after their payback period whereas others with a longer payback period can go on saving money for many years afterwards and so be much more cost-effective. It can mean that projects are prioritised in terms of how long their payback period is rather than how much money they save overall, and can therefore lead to decisions that are not cost-effective.

Discounted payback

A more sophisticated payback method exists that takes into account the time value of money, and so provides a more accurate method of assessment. It is called discounted payback.

This method of calculating the payback period of a new system takes into account the fact that money received (or saved) in the future is worth less than money spent or received today. The discount rate used will be the same you use for other calculations. Table B in the Appendix is also used to convert future cash flows into present value terms.

The process is straightforward. The money saved each year is converted into its present value using Table B, and a running total is kept. Once this running total exceeds the initial cost of a project or system we have made a 'profit' and achieved payback. The following example should help clarify the process.

Suppose £1,000 is invested in energy efficient lighting and it saves £300 per year. For a company with a cost of capital of 4 per cent a table would be set out as below. The 'present value' column is the £300 multiplied by the relevant factor from Table B.

As you can see the project would achieve payback in four years' time. If we had used 'simple payback' and divided £1,000 by £300 it would suggest that payback would be achieved in just over three years' time.

Year	Factor from Table B	Present value	Running total
1	0.96	288	288
2	0.92	276	564
3	0.89	267	831
4	0.85	255	1,086

Built Asset Management

The term built asset management (BAM) is in less common usage than others such as property management or maintenance management, hence it is important to establish what it means, both generally and in the context of this book. BAM has been defined by property professionals as being the maintenance and refurbishment of the building fabric, its services and immediate surroundings (hence it encompasses maintenance management and has a close relationship with property management). What such a definition lacks, however, is any indication of the *purpose* of BAM. It can be argued that the lack of attention to this aspect is one of the reasons for the 'Cinderella' role that the activity has, until recently, played. The reason for carrying out maintenance and refurbishment is not to produce the most immaculate accommodation possible; it is rather to keep buildings and sites at an *appropriate* standard for the organisation in occupation. This view of BAM is informed by the recent growth of **facilities management** (FM). Hence this chapter takes the following view of BAM:

Built asset management seeks to provide a cost-effective service that:

- keeps the building stock appropriate for organisational needs;
- creates and maintains an *acceptable* physical environment (legal and organisational minima – fitness for purpose, H&S, security, etc);
- creates and maintains a *desirable* environment (effect on the user – comfort, convenience, pleasure, productivity, etc);
- creates and maintains a relationship with the wider community (jobs, transport, crime, image, waste, etc).

The consequence of the above is that BAM should be viewed, not merely as an overhead or on-cost, but rather from the point of view of its effects on the 'core' business (ability to respond to change, working processes, protection of investment in property, etc).

This chapter will focus on the management of maintenance and refurbishment of the building fabric (excluding building services, which are the subject of Chapter 1, and landscaping/external works) and the relationship of these activities with the organisation occupying the accommodation and the individual building users. It will not be possible in this short piece to consider the legislative framework in which BAM operates, although at an operational level a knowledge of health and safety and employment legislation is particularly important. Before considering maintenance management it is necessary to analyse the more fundamental issues of obsolescence and quality. The chapter will then go on to address data requirements and issues related to users (customer service). Finally, BAM will be considered in the broader context of property portfolio management and regeneration.

Building 'life' and obsolescence

The built environment can be subdivided into layers which have different characteristics. Various terms have been coined for these layers, most recently by Stewart Brand, building on a model proposed by leading workplace consultant, Frank Duffy (see the appropriate reading list in Appendix 2 at the end of the book). These layers differ, not just in their physical components and the professional groups which design and manage them, but also in terms of their intended permanence and amenability to change. Hence each layer has a different 'life'. It is important to distinguish between *actual* life and *designed* life; the former is the result of obsolescence, which may have other causes than physical breakdown. Obsolescence will be discussed at greater length later in the chapter; for the moment it is useful to consider the six layers (each beginning with the letter 's') which Brand identifies in terms of their likely *actual* lives; this will highlight some of the factors which influence obsolescence.

The *site* is the most fundamental, in the sense that its geographical location is unchanging. What happens *around* it, however, may affect its suitability for a particular function (changes in road pattern, adjoining uses/built form, public transport, pollution, etc), and what happens *on* it, in terms of landscaping, pedestrian routes and car parking (although outside the scope of this chapter), has a great impact on the perception of the building by users, customers and the general public; it is also relatively easy to change.

The *structure* (the load-bearing elements of the building) is generally difficult and expensive to change, and hence usually has a life of between 30 and 60 years (sometimes much longer).

The *skin* (external surfaces) will probably last about 20 years before being remodelled because of fashion, technology or as part of a large-scale refurbishment.

Services may be subdivided into two major categories. First are what might be termed 'building' services – heating and air-conditioning systems, lifts, plumbing, electrical wiring, etc. These are likely to be partially or totally renewed between 7 and 20 years as a result of image (eg sanitary and light fittings), technical advances (eg heating systems) or wear (eg hot water tanks). In buildings where the services are embedded in the structure replacement may be so difficult and costly as to jeopardise the future of the building itself. Secondly, communications systems (telecoms and computer networks) which have a much shorter life because of the rate of technological advance and are now often partially or totally replaced after three to five years.

The *space plan* refers to the interior in terms of partitions, suspended ceilings, doors, flooring, etc. Functional requirements and fashion result in some commercial offices replacing at least some of these elements after as little as three years, although in more stable settings they may last 30 years.

Finally there is *stuff,* the items that are moveable, although they may be connected to one of the other layers – furniture, telephones, photocopiers, desk lamps, plants, etc which may be owned or leased by the organisation in residence, and which also may have a life of only a few years.

Duffy and Brand also point out that if the cumulative costs are considered over the whole life of a building (say 50 years) the initial cost of the building is far outweighed by the cost of successive generations of *space plan, services* and *skin.* It can be seen, therefore, that although, of the six 's's, this chapter focuses on *structure, skin* and *space plan,* the other layers (*site, services* and *stuff*) are related to, and have influence on, BAM.

Hence it can also be seen that the way in which maintenance and refurbishment is managed is driven not just by the inevitable physical decay of the fabric but also by organisational policy decisions, which are, in turn, influenced by a wider socio-economic agenda. What might be called the 'technical' view of BAM, which relates only to the physical artefacts, is much less acceptable in the current climate of integration, partnership and holistic thinking. The difficulty with this more complex model is deciding what the 'best' course of action is in any given situation. Hence, for major decisions like whether to refurbish a building, or to sell/demolish/

terminate the lease, **option appraisal** techniques may be employed. These seek to analyse future risk and uncertainties and to take into account the range of views about what is 'best' which arise as a result of the different cultures and values of those who have an interest in the outcome (often called 'stakeholders').

There is not space here for a detailed examination of option appraisal but it is significant in its connection to the need to make sustainable decisions. Such decisions can be defined as seeking to prevent (delay) obsolescence.

We saw from Brand's building layers that replacement decisions came about not just as a result of physical decay but also because of a failure to satisfy functional requirements. Hence a building can be said to have a socio-economic life as well as a physical one, and all or part of it can become functionally obsolescent as well as physically so. Furthermore, it can be seen that functional obsolescence is associated with user requirements, and may occur if a new user moves in, facets of the user's business change, or as a result of a change in user expectations. Whether functional or physical obsolescence actually results in replacement, however, is dependent upon the user's ability to tolerate the 'failed' component and the availability of finance. Furthermore, some components are likely to be replaced before failure as part of planned maintenance (see below). It can be seen, therefore, that data on the lifespans of *actual* components are not merely a record of physical failure, they may just as easily reflect policy or functional life.

Nevertheless, **life cycle** data are useful in predicting approximate timings and costs of future investment. Such data from your own stock of buildings are particularly useful as they will not only reflect local conditions but also provide information on the *reasons* for replacement. If local records do not exist published data will provide some guidance. The following provisos should be borne in mind when using life cycle data:

- The focus on capital cost, and the separation of capital and revenue budgets make an holistic, whole-life policy difficult.
- The uncertainty surrounding future events, costs, interest rates, etc means that life cycle costing, although useful, is only a 'best guess'.
- Different definitions of 'operating life' and 'running costs' can result in widely differing results.
- The predicted 'life' may assume optimum maintenance but with minimal or no maintenance the result may be very different (this

raises the question of whether the level of maintenance provision should be a consideration when components are being specified).
- The calculations are unlikely to take into account the physical difficulty and organisational disruption of component replacement.

A theoretical economic model would be of frequent minor maintenance interventions and more widely spaced major maintenance which lead to major refurbishment. This cycle would then be repeated until the cost of refurbishment exceeds that of demolition and replacement (or sale and move). In real situations the minor maintenance is sometimes neglected with the consequence that major work is necessary sooner. Furthermore, refurbishment may, as we have seen, be triggered by fashion or functional obsolescence rather than physical failure, or demolition may take place for political reasons. Finally, there is the influence of rising user expectations which means that returning the building to its original performance level is no longer acceptable.

The commonly voiced idea that higher initial costs lead to lower running costs and hence more economical buildings in the long term is an oversimplification. The picture is much more variable because it is affected not just by quality but also by complexity. Hence if the higher initial cost is a result of sophisticated services and components, although these *may* result in greater user satisfaction they *may* also have higher cleaning, maintenance and (in the case of services) running, costs than more basic provision. By implication greater complexity also results in a need for more management activity.

A feature of the 1990s was the tension, in many organisations, between a culture of constant change, driven mainly by cost cutting, which encourages short-term thinking, and a growth of interest in 'sustainability', which implies a long-term perspective. Furthermore, with regard to property and BAM, there are now high-profile 'virtual' companies organised around technology rather than places. Most businesses, however, will continue to need physical locations in the foreseeable future, albeit of a different and more flexible nature than in the past. In order to provide the efficient and effective accommodation (owned, leased, through partnership arrangements, etc) that is needed to support the business plan a property strategy (sometimes called estate or accommodation strategy) is required that plans for relocations, disposals, acquisitions and major refurbishments. The length of time the strategy covers (and the frequency with which it is reviewed) will depend on the type of business, but will probably be between 5 and 15 years. BAM should both *reflect* and *inform* the property strategy: *reflect* by carrying out minimal maintenance (health, safety and security only) on property set for disposal, for instance, and *inform* via feedback on the performance of the current stock. Both these activities imply an agreed set of BAM (predominantly maintenance) standards and performance indicators applicable in specified situations.

Standards and quality

An obvious way of choosing a product or a service is on price, but our everyday experience reveals that there is usually a balance between cost and 'quality'. This balance is implied by the term 'value for money' – the oft-quoted example of the Mini and the Rolls Royce both being value for money in spite of the difference in price. A further factor in this cost/performance equation is that of 'fitness for purpose' of the product or service, hence if a car is required that is easy to park in a city and economical in terms of fuel consumption these factors influence the choice. This demonstrates the *relative* nature of the concept of 'quality' and how different groups or individuals may disagree as to its definition.

Standards

Standards relate to quality in the sense that they are a level of performance (very often intended as a minimum, but sometimes treated as a maximum). Standards associated with BAM may have legal weight (through Acts of Parliament, Building Regulations, British/International Standards, etc); they may be set by other external bodies, eg those related to funding in the public sector (Housing Corporation, Higher Education Funding Council for England, etc); or they may be set by organisational policy. The term 'standard' tends to be used rather loosely and some 'standards' are, in fact, only good practice guidance. It may be seen that it is important to distinguish between these categories for reasons of legal liability, funding, internal accountability and the extent to which the 'standard' is open to modification by a department within an organisation. It is surprising how often individuals working in BAM are unclear as to which category a particular standard belongs.

BAM standards relate to both the physical and management aspects of the service.

Examples of physical standards:

- Fire, health and safety
- Condition/'fitness' of stock
- Performance/life/sustainability of building and components
- Thermal insulation/energy efficiency
- Space standards
- Ventilation/daylight/noise
- Facilities for people with disabilities

Examples of management standards:

- Speed of maintenance response times/job completion
- Quality of site workmanship
- Procedures for tenant involvement/feedback
- Speed of document 'throughput' (eg repair requests, invoices)
- Monitoring/quality assurance procedures
- Expertise/training of personnel (management and site)
- Information and equipment systems

From the above it can be seen that standards may be quantitative (eg area per user) or qualitative (eg repair workmanship) and may relate to the finished product (eg thermal insulation) or the process (eg document throughput).

Performance indicators

Performance indicators (PIs) are the organisation's performance measured against a 'standard' or target.

Characteristics of performance indicators:

- Measured against standards which are available to all involved and have been agreed by key personnel
- Used for both accountability (internally and externally) and good management
- Two categories: key indicators (for accountability) and secondary indicators (as management tools)
- Must be related to context (including factors beyond the control of the organisation)
- Customer involvement in feedback and setting targets is important
- Data collection – are the data useful enough to warrant the cost of collection?

If the performance falls short of the target there are two possible courses of action: improve the performance or revise the target (the latter is not an option where the target is a legal requirement).

Example key PIs for maintenance:

- Cost per sq.m. of floor space, or (better) per a measure of business output
- Expenditure against budget (response and planned maintenance)
- Maintenance backlog (average cost of outstanding repairs per building, site, department)
- % of jobs giving rise to customer complaints (and nature of complaint)
- % of jobs where remedial work needed
- Supervision/overhead costs as a % of total expenditure
- % of response times achieved by repair category
- % response maintenance compared to planned maintenance
- % of work not completed within identified cycles
- % of stock achieving specific standards (eg energy efficiency)

Secondary indicators may be subsets of the above, eg percentage with double glazing (in connection with planned programmes of replacement and energy efficiency), or related to the performance of departments or staff, eg percentage of invoices paid within seven days of receipt.

This leads us to a consideration of maintenance management in more detail.

Maintenance management and data requirements

The British Standard definition of maintenance (BS 3811: Terms Used in Terotechnology) is 'The combination of all technical and associated administrative actions intended to retain an item in, or restore it to, a state in which it can perform its required function'. This definition, by including 'function', relates maintenance to the purpose of the building and hence, indirectly, to users. The problem is that although it uses the word 'restore' which implies 'returning to original condition' the 'required function' will change over time, either because of a change of use or because of changing (usually rising) user expectations. Hence it is often difficult to draw the line between 'maintenance' and 'refurbishment' (this can sometimes be an advantage, however, as it allows flexibility in the management of budgets).

Maintenance may be divided into 'response' (sometimes called 'reactive' or 'day-to-day') and 'planned'.

Response maintenance

The essential characteristic of response maintenance is that it is initiated by the building user (as opposed to planned maintenance activity which is triggered by a 'professional' – Building Surveyor, Estates Manager, etc). A crucial part of the response process is the management of these repair requests; this will, therefore, be examined in some detail. The situation where minor repairs are carried out by a caretaker or 'odd job man' (multi-skilled employee) is less common today as a consequence of the trend of reducing staff numbers and outsourcing. The sequence of events will be considered, therefore, by taking a 'typical' situation where telephone requests from a group of sites/buildings are received by a help desk (which may just cover building maintenance but, in many organisations will deal with all 'facilities' type problems – cleaning, telephones, furniture, etc). Figure 4.1 shows the sequence in simplified form.

The process of deciding what work is required can be aided by a checklist of questions (often part of a computer program that prompts the help desk operator), information about the building(s), and details of work that has already been ordered, either through the response system or in the planned maintenance programme. This information can be available to the operator from an integrated database, which may include floor plans. The receiver of the request has to allocate the work to a priority category. These would typically be 'emergency', 'urgent' and 'normal' and would each have a response time given to them (eg 24 hours, one week, three weeks). There are two ways of deciding priority: it used to be common practice for a member of staff with a relatively high level of expertise to make a decision in each individual case; now, however, it is much more likely that the help desk operator has access to a computer system which generates the category automatically by a combination of the job description, the location and the user (certain locations, eg the production line in a factory, and users, eg frail elderly people, affect the seriousness of the fault). Which jobs are in which category and the exact response times should have been decided in negotiation with the building users (tenants, departments, etc) and should be reviewed periodically in the light of experience and customer feedback.

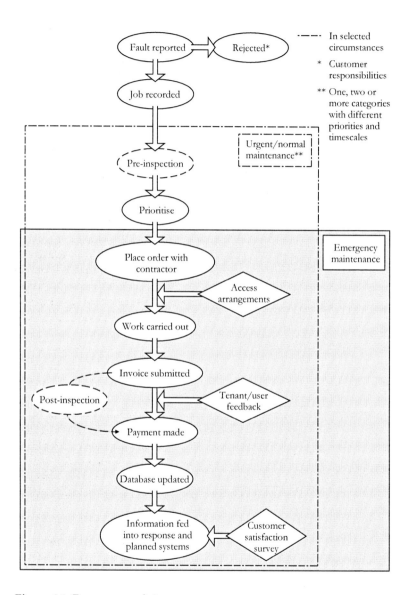

Figure 4.1 Response maintenance processes

In order to be able to analyse response maintenance to determine patterns, it is necessary to record information in addition to priority. Details such as the nature of the repair, the location and reason for the fault, and the contractor to which it is assigned can be recorded by numerical codes or key words. The system must allow reports to be generated according to any of these parameters, in addition to those which feature in the general database to which it is linked – user name and type, site, building, etc (these will be default codes generated automatically from the address). These details can highlight problem areas, and hence inform future management, planned maintenance and investment

The receiver of the request will log the work, give the complainant a unique reference number for the job, check access arrangements and, where budgets are devolved to departments, assign the applicable charging code. If a **schedule of rates** is being used then a provisional cost can be generated at this stage (this aids financial management in terms of recording 'committed' expenditure). The order is then sent to the appropriate contractor or member of in-house staff for action. A pre-inspection of the problem may be necessary in some circumstances. These will vary according to the particular organisation but would include indications of serious or more general problems, eg brickwork cracks in horizontal joints coinciding with wall tie positions. Good practice suggests that about 10 per cent of jobs should be inspected *after the work is complete* to check compliance with the specification. When the invoice for the work is submitted this should be checked against the job description that was logged when the request was received. This is because the actual work carried out needs to be recorded in order to keep an accurate maintenance history. Any discrepancy could have arisen as a result of the user not realising the exact nature of the work, the help desk recording it inaccurately or the contractor making an error. Hence a percentage of these cases should be checked to determine the source of the discrepancy in order to review practice and check performance.

Finally, it is important to link to the job record the user feedback (simple forms to be completed immediately after the work is done) and to ensure that more general surveys of customer satisfaction of the maintenance service are conducted periodically (once or twice a year). These should be used when planning for the future (in conjunction with the maintenance records) in order to ensure that the focus of maintenance is to support the core business (eg in reviewing contractor performance the quality of the physical job and the degree of disruption to users need to be taken into account).

A major problem with response maintenance is cost control. Because by its very nature response maintenance is unpredictable

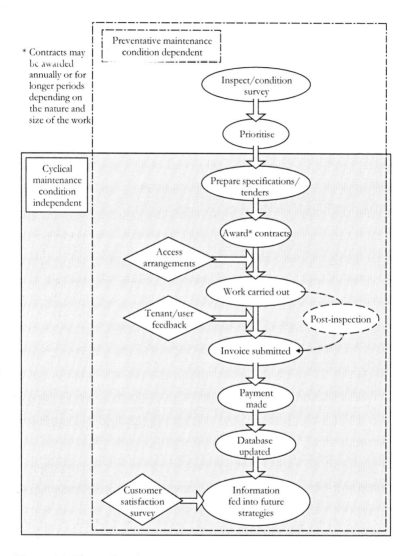

Figure 4.2 Planned maintenance processes

and was often, in the past, carried out on a 'jobbing' or daywork basis ensuring value for money was difficult. The public sector was affected in the 1980s by a series of reports by the Audit Commission on maintenance and asset/property management of housing, education and local government buildings. The recommendation was to increase the percentage of the maintenance budget spent on planned maintenance to about 60 per cent on the basis that this would provide better cost control, reduce disturbance and improve management of the service. Hence the trend in the public sector in the late 1980s and early 1990s was generally to reduce the proportion of response maintenance and increase that of planned. The growth of fragmentation, however (local management of schools, transfer of housing stock from local authorities to housing associations, changes in NHS trusts, etc), combined with a trend for outsourcing has led to a situation where a variety of organisations hold information on, and have an interest in, the maintenance/ built asset management of buildings but few have either the total picture or the certainty of continued involvement in the long term. Such a situation is less conducive to the sustained investment implied by planned maintenance and has resulted, with the low level of finance available, in a halt to this trend in some organisations. The **Private Finance Initiative** and **Public–Private Partnerships** are designed to tackle this problem, providing immediate investment, long-term funding and a blurring of the division between the 'public' and 'private' sectors. In the private sector itself, the drivers of maintenance management have been statutory compliance, staff health and safety (and only in some cases comfort and well-being) and, most importantly, continuance of the core business. Hence in some sectors, like retail, techniques used for manufacturing and stock control such as 'just-in-time' have been applied to maintenance, particularly of the engineering services which can both be monitored and are central to the business (eg freezers).

Planned maintenance

Planned maintenance may be divided into 'cyclical' maintenance and 'preventative' maintenance (see Figure 4.2).

Cyclical maintenance consists of those regular activities that are carried out irrespective of the condition of the building/element. It is often governed by a legal requirement, eg lifts and gas installations. It can also encompass cyclical activity like repainting where this is carried out independently of a condition assessment.

In contrast, preventative maintenance is dependent on such a condition assessment (condition survey) being carried out by a person with some knowledge of building, usually a professional building surveyor. The type of survey will depend on the nature of the stock. If this consists of a collection of unique buildings, then each will need to be surveyed, but if there are elements of repetition (factory units, housing, etc) then a sample will suffice. In either case, a rolling programme of inspections ensures continuity of work and regular updating of survey data (typically every five years, as in quinquennial surveys of ecclesiastical buildings). Although called 'condition' surveys these visits are often used to collect information on factors other than pure 'condition' for a variety of reasons:

- **Establishing condition** – this may be expressed in a number of ways, eg on a scale from unacceptable to excellent, expenditure required, remaining 'life'. It is usually done by element (eg windows, external walls) but there may be occasions when it is necessary to give the whole building or site an overall condition.

- **Establishing attributes** – this relates to the actual *form* of the elements of the building/site eg *tiled* roof, and would include *materials*, eg *concrete*.

- **Quantifying stock by construction type** – in order to highlight possible problems (eg with large concrete panel or timber frame constructions of the 1960s), and, in a large stock, in order to select a stratified sample which is representative of the range of construction types in the property estate.

- **Forecasting repair needs** – in order to plan future resource requirements in terms of loans, sinking funds, staffing levels, etc. This information feeds into the property strategy by informing decisions about disposals.

- **Preparing planned preventative maintenance programmes** – repair or replacement by element (eg asphalt roofs on all, or a proportion of, the stock), or by building (eg major work to the whole of a building or group of buildings).

- **Assessing potential improvements** – there is often an element of improvement in planned preventative maintenance, eg single glazed windows being replaced with double glazed, but this heading refers to larger-scale improvements where facilities are upgraded, eg kitchens. Such refurbishments may involve structural alterations connected with replanning the way the building operates, either because of a change in user function or because of rising user expectations.

- **Carrying out an energy audit** – as a result of concerns over energy efficiency (both from the point of view of future expenditure and image) and/or funding requirements (eg Housing Corporation).

- Stock valuation.
- Providing evidence for funding application/transfer of ownership/partnership agreements.

This possible breadth of scope, the range of expertise required, and the inherent difficulties in managing the process can lead to problems, the most common of which are listed below:

- **Collecting too much data** – there is a temptation to collect more data than is needed – what might be called the 'while-you're-there-you-might-as-well' syndrome. This should be resisted. The purposes for which the data will be used need to be considered carefully in order that the 'reports' generated by the survey support the management and decision structures. The level of detail should be restricted to that which is absolutely necessary.

- **Inadequate training and monitoring** – even when staff are appropriately qualified and have had general experience of condition surveys there is a need for training related to the particular survey. Similarly quality checks should be carried out of survey and data transfer accuracy and completion, as well as progress and financial monitoring.

- **Raising expectations of tenants/users** – the very act of inspection is likely to suggest that work will be carried out, unless the purposes of the survey are discussed and the decision-making process explained to tenants or users (who, preferably, will have some input into which data are collected and how they are used).

- **A lack of understanding**:
  - that the detailed repair programming is a separate exercise;
  - of the resource implications of the survey itself.

- **Revealing immediate repair needs for which there is no budget** – although aimed primarily at preventative maintenance and long-term planning, if emergency or very urgent items of repair are identified by the surveyors (that have gone unnoticed or unreported by users) these will require immediate attention.

- **Compatibility of software systems** – condition surveys are often carried out by consultants who offer a total service and have their own computer systems; alternatively the in-house team may use an off-the-peg software system to capture (via hand-held computers) and analyse data. In either case compatibility with other systems (eg for response maintenance) is important (if a bespoke system is being designed the links with existing systems are of great importance).

The brief for the survey is an accepted part of the process when consultants are employed, but is important even for in-house staff in order to make maximum use of resources. Integration with existing systems should allow the maximum possible information to be given to the surveyors in advance (these might include building/site locations, plans, photographs, construction details, a request to investigate the cause of a recurrent problem which has been identified from the record of response maintenance, etc). Photographs are particularly useful and relatively inexpensive: surveyors should be asked to take general and detailed photographs (the advent of digital cameras has made integrating these with other information much easier). Similar good practice guidelines apply whether data capture is computerised or manual.

In order to produce a planned maintenance programme the surveyors' judgements contained in the condition survey need to be combined with various other considerations. One of these is the creation of packages of work (eg if expensive scaffolding is required to repair a particular element and there are items suggested for work next year which would also require this scaffolding, are the savings in cost and disruption associated with doing all the work this year and none next justifiable in terms of the consequent delay of other possible work?). Another is to spread expenditure as evenly as possible over the years of the programme to ensure controlled spending and a continuing workload for in-house staff or contractors (unless there are any particular one-off grants or funding arrangements for particular programmes, eg for energy efficiency improvements). There will also be considerations of organisational policy (eg a decision to have a programme of *replacement*, rather than *repair*, of a component because of the poor condition of most examples), and the degree of disruption to tenants/users (taking into account the possibilities for decanting). Such decisions are usually made by managers on the basis of experience, but some computer programs enable modelling of 'what if' scenarios, which will help with this process.

Maintenance costs

Hence it can be seen that the cost of maintenance is affected by both the nature of the physical stock and the form of management:

Characteristics of the stock affecting maintenance costs:
- Condition
- Type (and complexity) of construction
- Physical form and ease of access
- Age
- Location

Management factors affecting maintenance costs:
- Organisational policy
- Required quality of work – the quality or 'level' of maintenance that is specified depends on:
  - available finance
  - desired image of building
  - expected 'life' of building
  - revenue earning capacity of building
  - use/function of building
  - construction characteristics
  - legal requirements of health and safety, and considerations of security
- Function/use
- Characteristics of the workforce

Maintenance data

An **asset register** forms the basis of data for maintenance; it is to this that condition, response and other maintenance data relates. It also provides the base data on property from which to calculate measures, like space utilisation, that bring together property and general 'business' data (eg details of tenants/users and financial data). The asset register may include site as well as building data.

Site data might include:

- a unique reference number;
- location (OS grid reference, possibly related to a computerised geographical information system, that allows the user to switch between different scales to show the building, site and more general location);
- type and nature of tenure (eg length of lease, break clauses, period of rent review);
- area;
- legal restraints (restrictive covenants, rights of way, tree preservation orders, boundaries/adjoining owners, planning restrictions on access points, in a conservation area, etc);

- physical features (eg bearing capacity, water table, location of services)

It might also record details of the surrounding area in terms of facilities, transport, etc.

Building data might include:

- reference and/or address;
- gross area (the area within the external walls) and the net lettable area(s) (for rent or lease purposes, it excludes major circulation) (for management purposes it is also necessary to have data on cleaning area, department area, etc);
- construction type;
- component information;
- year of construction (not age, which needs to be updated every year);
- 'as built' drawings;
- condition (at last survey);
- use/occupants (function, department(s), etc);
- fire precautions;
- legal restraints (eg party wall agreements, liquor licence, maximum occupancy, etc);
- degree of access for people with disabilities.

Customer service

It has been emphasised already in this chapter that the purpose of built asset management is to support the core business of the organisation (manufacturing, housing, etc) and user feedback and customer surveys have been mentioned in connection with maintenance. Users are not a homogeneous group, however; not only will there almost certainly be differences between the views of senior management and the 'shopfloor' but also between individuals because of their personalities and previous experiences.

Post-occupancy evaluation

Post occupancy evaluation (POE) is a technique to evaluate a building after it has been occupied in order to determine whether or not it fulfils the original brief or the needs of the current users. Emphasis is usually placed on the interaction between the building and its user organisation or social group, and the individuals who make up that group.

The range of techniques and methodologies employed in POEs is wide, but most apply a systematic approach in order to determine how effective and efficient the building is in use. The reasons for carrying out a POE might include:

- a recognition of the complexity and significance of the interrelationships between people, the physical environment and the organisation;
- acknowledgment that an organisation's built estate is as much a resource as its human and financial assets, and that the proactive management of the built estate can contribute significantly to the achievement of an organisation's goals;
- the need to demonstrate value for money by assessing whether a building 'works';
- the need, in the commercial office sector, to assess user requirements at a time of rapid organisational and technological change. In this context, pre-occupancy evaluations may play an increasingly effective role.

It has been suggested by Preiser *et al.* (see further reading) that a post-occupancy evaluation has a number of uses in that it:

- constitutes a proactive, not reactive, management approach;
- addresses the big picture not piecemeal actions;
- allows objective review of the situation;
- provides (a) rationale and support for budget allocation;
- is participative and therefore assists in implementing needed change;
- provides expertise not available 'in-house'.

Factors commonly included in post-occupancy evaluations are:

- economic;
- the effect of time;
- technical/environmental, for example:
  - fire safety;
  - structure;
  - building services;
- functional/administrative, for example:
  - workflow;
  - flexibility;
  - change;
- behavioural, for example:
  - socio/psychological;

- privacy/interaction;
- perception.

Although POEs can be large complex exercises, most, because of restricted resources, are of an 'indicative' nature only. An indicative POE would probably include:

- archive and document evaluation, including space utilisation schedules and H&S records;
- evaluation by observation and questioning rather than measurement;
- performance issues (questions to the client organisation's management);
- expert 'walk-through' evaluation;
- interviews with *selected* users;
- performance criteria based on the evaluation team's experience.

Organisations are most likely to carry out POEs if there is a particular problem that could potentially affect productivity, eg a suspicion of sick building syndrome.

Characteristics of 'good' buildings

Several studies by Adrian Leaman (a sociologist) and Bill Bordass (an expert on building services) (both have chapters in a book by Duffy, Laing and Crisp – see further reading) have identified a number of factors which characterise the buildings which rate highly in user surveys, the 'best' buildings:

1 Optimise relationships between physical and human systems over their lifetimes.
2 Keep resource inputs and undesirable effects to the necessary minimum.
3 Are simple but capable of upgrading, avoiding unnecessary complexity.
4 Are economical of time in operation.
5 Respond rapidly to change.
6 Have sufficient management resources to deal with both routine requirements and unpredictable consequences of physical or behavioural complexity.
7 Are comfortable and safe most of the time, but use properties 5 and 6 if difficulties occur.
8 Try to avoid introducing failure pathways.

BAM should aim to support organisations in achieving accommodation with these characteristics.

Context

The relationship between BAM and property management was referred to at the start of this chapter. The management of the portfolio of property of an organisation may encompass a variety of forms of tenure: sole ownership, co-ownership (as in cooperative workshops), leasing, etc. The speed of change in the business world has led to many organisations seeking increasing flexibility in their property portfolios. Hence the use of such arrangements as sale and leaseback which relieve the organisation of the ties of ownership and allow, through frequent break clauses, the opportunity to move or renegotiate conditions. It can be seen that in a climate of such diversity and change the role of BAM mentioned earlier to both *reflect* and *inform* the property strategy becomes particularly important.

In the public sector the government has been encouraging public/private partnerships through the **Private Finance Initiative**, **Public–Private Partnerships**, and the 'New Deal' to attract private investment to public services like hospitals, schools, universities and housing. These schemes are an attempt at regeneration both by addressing the current poor condition of many public sector buildings, and by trying to protect their future. In so doing the aim is to reduce the risk to the public purse, hence connecting with political agendas about value for money (characterised as 'best value'). Part of this is an attitude to procurement which moves away from accepting the lowest bid by trying to take more qualitative and stakeholder issues (as in the 'New Deal for Communities') into account – in other words an attempt to shift the goal from *efficiency* towards *effectiveness*. In practice reaching agreements in which each partner achieves its aims (which for the private partner will include making a profit) has sometimes proved difficult and the rate of take-up of these schemes has been slower than the government hoped. The reasons such arrangements are important for BAM, however, are partly that they involve consideration of property over its whole life (connecting to ideas of sustainability and energy efficiency) and partly because they have implications for the manner in which BAM is organised and managed.

The business plan of the organisation, of which the BAM function is part, will help to determine the direction and aims of the service. Also any quality initiatives it has embraced, like the international quality standard, ISO 9000, Total Quality Management or Business Excellence programmes, will affect the management procedures employed. There will also be external constraints and incentives in the form of town and country planning restrictions, special area grants and tax relief schemes. Hence it can be seen that BAM has a part to play in the delivery of organisational goals.

Chapter 5

Workspace: Design and Evaluation

The design and utilisation of space is a key area in the management of the workplace. The sole point of occupying the building in the first place is to provide a controlled space in which production can be most efficiently undertaken. The purchase or lease of property usually makes up the largest portion of a company's fixed costs, and yet is often managed poorly despite the expense involved and the high cost of each square metre of space.

Architects and building designers respond to the needs of their clients and undertake to provide what is specified although there has been a tendency to provide companies with 'standardised' designs, if for no other reason than that they are cheaper than designing unusual 'one-off' buildings, and most firms prefer to economise on how much they spend on their premises. However, once the building has been handed over to the occupier it is up to them to make the best of it. Buildings very rarely end their life looking the same as when they were built, especially as they may be put to fifty or eighty years of hard service. During that time they may be extended, refurbished, have internal walls added or demolished, have elements replaced (such as windows) or have components **retrofitted** such as mechanical ventilation, and may be occupied by a succession of different firms with different needs, providing different products and services. Because there is such a huge range of commercial activity that can take place in a building – everything from heavy industry to a sports centre – it is not feasible to provide a step-by-step guide that is equally useful to everybody and which covers every possible variation of business from a steel mill to a hotel. Instead we will look at key principals, and use the model of an office environment as an example. Office space, especially when located in the central business district, tends to be among the most expensive of all business premises, and so naturally enough a considerable amount of time, thought and effort has been devoted to its efficient utilisation. The lessons learned can be applied (in general terms) to other kinds of business premises and can provide useful ideas that can be adopted and adapted.

There have been many studies commissioned over the years into the demands of office users and the productivity of office developers. One almost universal finding is that firms are demanding more flexible space, and space that can be adapted to the needs of the latest innovations in IT. Producers of office space have, until very recently, been slow to respond to these changing patterns of demand. New offices have most often been supplied to the standardised designs available from most construction companies and property developers. This 'off the peg' approach is starting to become a thing of the past. Rapid changes in corporate culture, work patterns, technology, energy costs and environmental awareness means that producers are having to become far more responsive to changing patterns of demand. Downsizing, mergers, relocations and reorganisations mean that the last thing businesses want is inflexible, static space, and recent innovations in office design are starting to acknowledge this. In this chapter we will look at how office space can be utilised most effectively. The chapter will be divided into three sections. Firstly, we will consider how new premises may best be commissioned, and look at the advantages and disadvantages of different procurement routes. Secondly we will look at how space can be organised cost-effectively, whether it is new-build or the reorganisation of existing space. Finally we will look again at the topic of post-occupancy evaluation, which is a rapidly growing service provided by building professionals to ensure the long-term cost effective use of space.

New premises

Building professionals use the term 'procurement' when discussing the purchase of new premises. There are three main ways of doing this, known as the 'traditional method', 'management contracting' and 'design and build'. Each of these has advantages and dis-advantages and there is no one best method; it depends on the type of space you want as to which route is the best.

Although a full discussion of the relative merits of all three systems could easily fill a book on its own it is perfectly possible to give a brief summary of the main features of each, and we will begin with the traditional method.

The traditional method gets its name by default – it has simply been around the longest and in comparison the other two methods are relative newcomers, not really making significant inroads until the 1980s. The traditional method works as follows. You (the client) approach an architect to design your new premises. Once these designs are complete the construction of the project is put out to tender, which means that construction companies look at the architect's designs and make an offer as to how much they will charge to undertake the work. Once a bid has been accepted (usually the lowest bid, perhaps depending on the reputation of the company) the construction company builds the property under the supervision and guidance of the architect, and all three parties sign a contract detailing their rights and responsibilities. The standard contract is called JCT 80 (drawn up by the Joint Contract Tribunal in 1980). The architect is paid a fee which is usually a percentage of the cost of the building.

Its chief advantage is one of competition. All the firms bidding for the work have the architect's detailed plans in front of them when preparing their tender, and are aware that their competitors have the same information to hand, so coming somewhere close to the economist's ideal of 'perfect competition'. Each firm has therefore the keenest possible incentive to bid a low price for the job, and they can base their bid on precise, detailed design information.

The disadvantage is one of the separation of design and construction. Although this allows for competition it also can lead to poor communication. The construction company has had no input into the original design, and the architect has no statutory right to control their construction process (although he or she will certainly be on hand to consult, monitor and advise). This separation of function means that any changes or amendments in the design during the construction phase can be very time-consuming and expensive.

Because of these problems other methods have evolved, and one of the earliest deviations from the traditional method was the management contract approach which first appeared in the 1970s. Under this system a specialised construction management company is appointed by the client to oversee and supervise in the construction process on site. The construction work itself is rarely done by one contractor. It is usually split into several 'packages' and different companies bid to undertake each package (a package may be, for instance, the provision of the foundations, or the installation of a building's electrical systems). Each of these subcontractors will work under the overall direction of the management company, who usually undertake to provide common site facilities such as canteens, works offices and night security. The management company is usually paid a percentage of the 'prime cost', that is the sum of the costs of each 'package'.

There is no fixed rule for where the design of the building comes into the process. Sometimes detailed drawings may be completed by the management company. More commonly the management company undertakes to provide a 'starter' design that meets with the client's approval and to keep as close to this as possible during the construction process.

The advantage of the contract management system is that it does not separate the design and construction phases of a building as sharply as the traditional method does. Under the traditional method the design is undertaken in detail, followed by construction, which is time-consuming. The contract management system gets the process underway a lot quicker because work can be undertaken on site even before the design is finalised, which clearly saves time and money. It also offers more flexibility; as the design is rarely 100 per cent complete before construction begins it is far easier to add, change or modify elements during the construction process, which is more expensive to do under the traditional method.

Its disadvantage is that costs are not as clearly foreseeable as they are with the traditional route. Although costs can vary with the traditional route they are unlikely to do so by very much (as long as the client sticks with the original design). As the project management system usually begins with only an initial, sometimes embryonic design it is not as easy to be certain of the finished product, and there is in consequence a greater likelihood of overspending.

Because of the problems with these two methods many clients have turned to the design and build package in an attempt to both cut completion times and control costs with a greater degree of certainty. The design and build route is self-explanatory. It provides a 'one-stop-shop' for a client who will engage a single contractor to design, manage and construct the whole project from initial sketch designs to the final coat of paint on the front door. Its appeal is straightforward in that it cuts out the split between design and construction and also gives a fixed, set price for the finished project. There are many variants and hybrids of the 'core' design and build package, such as the appointment of the architect by the client rather than the contractor (known as novation), but they all have in common the offering of a 'package deal' with a single point of contact for the client. Its disadvantages are anecdotal because they rely on aesthetic opinion, but some clients (and especially their architects) argue that the finished product is often not very stylish because the need to cut costs and keep to tight budgets can put the architect in a subservient role where design ideas are compromised in favour of speed and efficiency, the same criticism that has also been labelled at the contract management approach. It is hard to quantify 'design flare', but it is often compromised when the role of the architect is diminished.

Even building professionals are divided as to which of these three routes is the best. Defenders of each can point to examples of badly built or badly designed buildings carried out under the other two systems and stylish, functional, cost-effective buildings carried out under their own method. There is a tendency for clients to consider an architect-lead, traditional route when commissioning a building where style is important, such as a company HQ, and to go with one of the other routes when commissioning something 'off the shelf' such as a warehouse, but this is not a cast iron rule.

Cost-effective space

Flexibility is desirable in new-build premises, but existing premises can be modified through the building or demolishing of walls, refurbishments and extensions. One of the central decisions in managing space (whether newly commissioned or existing premises) is the choice between open plan, closed plan, or a hybrid. Each of these is shown in Figure 5.1.

Until recently most offices were closed plan; buildings were divided into discrete 'cells', each with their own separate lighting and heating controls, and each room would contain a more or less fixed number of people, usually with a bespoke workstation. This pattern is familiar to most people and has worked well for many years. Recently, however, there has been a move toward open-plan office space, and as its advantages and disadvantages involve assessing how it compares to closed-plan office space we can examine the merits (and problems) of both types simply by examining open-plan workspace.

Open-plan workspace evolved from a desire to put more people into a given area and allow greater scope for moving them around in different combinations. Simply removing walls creates more space and clearly allows the same area to be used in a greater variety of ways. Despite the sometimes long-winded explanations offered in textbooks this is the main reason for the evolution of open-plan space.

The disadvantages are equally straightforward. Firstly they are often unpopular with staff who feel they are having their privacy

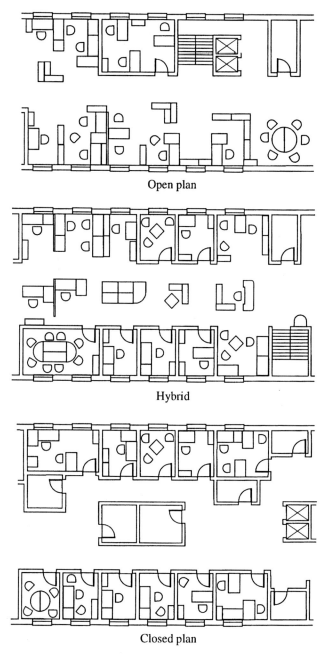

Open plan

Hybrid

Closed plan

Figure 5.1 Management of space

eroded and are being subjected to a greater degree of monitoring and scrutiny. This is reinforced in the cases where managers insist on the benefits of open-plan space for their staff while ensuring they have private 'traditional' offices for themselves. There is also a problem with noise and extra 'traffic' through the office area which can be a constant distraction and hinder productivity, although on the other hand staff often have much quicker access to each other – they simply need to walk across the room rather than to a separate suite of offices. The problem of noise is recognised as a legitimate one by office designers and a variety of strategies have been developed to deal with it. At their most simple they simply involve using noise absorbent components and materials. Thick carpet is good at absorbing sound, and ceilings can be designed (both in their shape and choice of materials) to absorb rather than reflect sound. At the 'hi tech' end of the scale are sound masking devices which are placed on the ceiling and which transmit sound waves at the same wavelength as the human voice so that they 'cancel out' the sound, much like two waves in your bathtub hitting each other head on and each subsiding to a small ripple. This might sound curious, but it has a long pedigree and a proven track record, being installed, for instance, in the offices of Willis Insurance Company in Ipswich in the mid-1970s, one of the first modern open-plan buildings in Britain, designed by Sir Norman Foster and already enjoying 'Listing' status usually reserved for much older pieces of outstanding architecture.

The other disadvantages of open-plan offices are less easily dealt with. Firstly you must consider heating and lighting costs in a 'flexitime' world. If two or three staff come in on Sunday and occupy an open plan office that usually has fifty staff, then the whole space has to be heated. Under the closed-plan system it is just one small office. Secondly, should a fire break out on the premises there is clear evidence that it spreads faster in an open space. Closed, separated rooms clearly act as firebreaks and slow down the spread of flame.

An increasingly popular alternative is to have a hybrid system containing elements of both, although it is usually discussed under the umbrella of open plan in many texts.

Such systems consist of panelling that can be fitted to brackets fixed to the wall and ceiling, so creating rooms of a variety of shapes and sizes. Should a new layout be devised the panels can be moved in the space of a few hours and so convert one large space to several small spaces or vice versa. There is not an infinite range of options available because the panels can only go where the brackets are, but as they are usually laid out in a grid across the whole work area it leaves enough permutations available for all but the most unusual space requirements. Although such systems cost more than simply building walls with bricks and mortar they offer a huge advantage in long-term flexibility. There is no firm rule here. The more likely you are to want to reorganise your workspace over the long term the more cost-effective such panel systems will be. If you are more or less happy with the space you have they are an unnecessary expense. Shop around if you decide you do want such a system as there is a wide range available, with big price differences between the top and bottom ends of the market.

Post-occupancy evaluation

Post-occupancy evaluation does exactly what it says – the evaluation of a building's performance after it has been occupied and used for a period of time. More and more firms are finding that such an evaluation can be good value for money, especially firms with large and complex estates. Buildings represent extremely large capital investments, and require a large amount of upkeep and maintenance over many years, usually over many decades. In these circumstances it is reasonable to make sure they are being used in the best, most cost-effective way. A post-occupancy evaluation will be undertaken by a professional with considerable building expertise, usually an architect, surveyor, or facilities manager, and can be on any scale from a one-day overview to an intensive analysis over an extended period of time.

The scale, technical sophistication and organisational complexity of buildings mean that it is difficult for the non-professional to fully and completely understand how they work and how different aspects of building management overlap. Buildings contain different structural materials, different service systems and a range of different people undertaking different tasks, all of which interact with each other, cost money, use space and are subject to a range of different legal restrictions and overlapping regulatory obligations. It is no wonder that they contain the potential for mismanagement and inefficiency, and with any but the smallest premises there is usually scope for rationalisation and improvement.

The scope of post-occupancy evaluation

There is no 'off-the-peg' format for post-occupancy evaluations. They can be tailored to fit individual building types and can come in a variety of formats. There are three principal areas that will be studied, three main timescales and two types of data. All of these overlap in different combinations but we can get an overall idea of what goes on by a brief summary of each of these aspects.

The three principal areas to be considered are the building's technical, functional and behavioural performance. The building's technical success will be assessed in terms of the performance of its structure, fabric and services against predetermined criteria, often though not exclusively regulatory. Such an assessment can be very straightforward – does the building conform to the Fire Regulations, do the walls conform to the U-values of Part L of the Building Regulations, and so forth. The final report can be used as the basis for legal action should a recently completed building be in breach of building codes. There can also be an assessment of performance quality that is not legally mandatory but still desirable. Is the building energy-efficient? Does the double glazing lead to overheating in summer? Does the air-conditioning system provide the necessary humidity control in IT areas? These are all technical questions, but clearly have implications for the building's functional and behavioural performance.

The functional aspects of a building are more subjective than its technical aspects, but are still vital to its proper functioning. They include such things as communication between different departments, access and security, and the identification of 'traffic flow' problems in the corridors and workspace. These are often managed and understood by the building users themselves, but an outsider with a 'fresh pair of eyes', especially when trained in building design, can often pick up points that have been missed, misunderstood or not managed to the maximum advantage.

The behavioural aspects of a building are perhaps the most subjective of all, but the fact that something is hard to measure does not mean it is unimportant. At its most simple it can include such basic questions as whether the building is comfortable to work in or not. 'Sick building syndrome' has been linked principally to heavily serviced buildings, but there is no doubt that drab, badly lit, poorly aired buildings of any kind can fit the pattern. No one works well in a building that is uncomfortable – too hot or too cold for instance – and the simple provision of a comfortable, pleasant workspace can improve working conditions significantly. Behavioural analysis can also examine areas such as density of workspace and the relative privacy of employees. The boss who insists that open-plan office space is the best thing since sliced bread and then insists on an office of their own is unlikely to contribute much to morale.

Neither the technical, functional or behavioural aspects of a building exist in a vacuum. At first glance you may think there is little overlap between a building's technical and behavioural aspects, but it is commonly greater than many people imagine. For instance, many studies show that staff who have direct control over the temperature, ventilation and lighting controls in their own workspace are happier in their work than those staff who have such things controlled for them by the unseen hand of management. Even more obvious is the link between functional and behavioural aspects; the layout of rooms (especially in open-plan workspaces) is a very important question to the people who spend 40 hours a week working in them, and managers who do not consult the opinions of their staff are simply stockpiling ill-will for the future.

Evaluations tend to look at short-, medium- and long-term aspects of building use, although as with technical, functional and behavioural analysis these will blend seamlessly into one another rather than being discrete and separate. Most organisations are principally concerned with short- and medium-term evaluations, although large organisations with significant real estate assets have a stronger financial incentive to conduct longer-term evaluations.

A short-term evaluation may typically take place within a year or two of a building's initial occupancy. Its role is to highlight (and suggest remedies for) immediate problems and to identify the potential for immediate improvements. If the building is new then this report will highlight any technical shortcomings such as faulty air conditioning or inefficient boilers.

A medium-term evaluation will tend to focus on the need and/or ability of the building to adapt or change over time. Technology changes far quicker than the building that it goes into, as does the structure of organisations. Many firms occupy premises thirty, fifty or a hundred years old, and yet use the very latest technology and organisational methods. There may be problems in trying to combine the old and the very new. Flexitime, shift working, hot desking and home working all clearly have implications for building use. Technological changes such as IT and the air-conditioning systems that go with it are also going to affect both the technical and functional aspects of a building's use. Some buildings are far more flexible than others and can be put to a wide range of uses over several decades. There are, for instance, many early nineteenth-century textile mills and warehouses still in use as factories, workshops, offices, shops, art galleries and houses. This is because they provide wide open, well lit, well ventilated space that can have walls added, ceilings lowered (to take mechanical ventilation) and floors raised (to take IT cabling) and so are often more popular as offices than the closed-plan and relatively inflexible concrete office blocks of the 1960s, even though they are over a century older. The current emphasis among building designers is to emulate this ideal and provide flexible workspace, and the adaption of existing premises can save the considerable expense of relocation.

Long-term evaluations may look at buildings a decade or more after their occupation. It is a useful exercise in helping assess the **life cycle** cost of components and measuring the long-term costs of maintenance, repair and upkeep. Companies with a large stock of buildings all intended to serve roughly the same function (such as high street banks and supermarkets) can learn from the strengths and weaknesses of their existing building stock, and so avoid repeating expensive errors when acquiring new stock. The life of a building can be divided into five stages: planning, design, construction, occupancy and post-occupancy evaluation. Step five will then 'loop' around and be used in stages one and two of any new building. Such long-term and large-scale evaluations undoubtedly pay dividends, but they are usually only cost-effective for large-scale organisations and most firms find that short- and medium-term evaluations suit their needs perfectly well.

The information gathered by the evaluation will almost certainly be a mixture of quantitative and qualitative data. Quantitative data is clearly 'harder', and will relate to clearly defined variables – what is the temperature range of a room? what is the lighting level (measured in lux)? what is the noise level (measured in decibels)? If any of these are contrary to statutory minimums or maximums you clearly have a problem.

You should, however, appreciate that qualitative data ('are you satisfied with your workspace?') are probably going to be very closely linked to quantitative data. Unpopular workspaces are sometimes unpopular for no clear reason, or for one you cannot measure (such as not having a window), but it is more often the case that they are unpopular because of being too hot or too cold, too noisy, badly lit or ventilated by poorly serviced air conditioning. You should also be aware that qualitative data is also going to depend on who you ask. The office manager may be genuinely content with their workspace. This is because they have assigned themselves plenty of space, a brand new desk, an ergonomically designed chair at a cost of £350 and a window view. The temp behind the filing cabinet will have a different view.

In conclusion we can say that buildings are extremely expensive pieces of business equipment that will be used continuously for several decades. It is important that they are managed efficiently, and yet are not compromised too greatly in terms of their appearance and internal environment. Whether procuring new premises or re-evaluating and redesigning existing property, there are many options open to the management team, and this chapter should help you to make informed decisions.

Table A Compound interest table: for finding the future value of a current amount

					Discount rate					
t	*1%*	*2%*	*3%*	*4%*	*5%*	*6%*	*7%*	*8%*	*9%*	*10%*
1	1.01	1.02	1.03	1.04	1.05	1.06	1.07	1.08	1.09	1.10
2	1.02	1.04	1.06	1.08	1.10	1.12	1.14	1.17	1.19	1.21
3	1.03	1.06	1.09	1.12	1.16	1.19	1.23	1.26	1.30	1.33
4	1.04	1.08	1.13	1.17	1.22	1.26	1.31	1.36	1.41	1.46
5	1.05	1.10	1.16	1.22	1.28	1.34	1.40	1.42	1.54	1.61
6	1.06	1.13	1.19	1.27	1.34	1.42	1.50	1.59	1.68	1.77
7	1.07	1.15	1.23	1.32	1.41	1.50	1.61	1.71	1.83	1.95
8	1.08	1.17	1.27	1.37	1.48	1.59	1.72	1.85	1.99	2.14
9	1.09	1.20	1.30	1.42	1.55	1.69	1.84	2.00	2.17	2.36
10	1.10	1.22	1.34	1.48	1.63	1.79	1.97	2.16	2.37	2.59
11	1.12	1.24	1.38	1.54	1.71	1.90	2.10	2.33	2.58	2.85
12	1.13	1.27	1.43	1.60	1.80	2.01	2.25	2.52	2.81	3.14
13	1.14	1.29	1.47	1.67	1.89	2.13	2.41	2.72	3.07	3.45
14	1.15	1.32	1.51	1.73	1.98	2.26	2.58	2.94	3.34	3.80
15	1.16	1.35	1.56	1.80	2.08	2.40	2.76	3.17	3.64	4.18
16	1.17	1.37	1.60	1.87	2.18	2.54	2.95	3.43	3.97	4.59
17	1.18	1.70	1.65	1.95	2.29	2.69	3.16	3.70	4.33	5.05
18	1.20	1.43	1.70	2.03	2.41	2.85	3.38	4.00	4.72	5.56
19	1.21	1.46	1.75	2.11	2.53	3.03	3.62	4.32	5.14	6.12
20	1.22	1.49	1.81	2.19	2.65	3.21	3.87	4.06	5.60	6.73

Table B **Present value table: for finding the present value of single future cashflow**

					Discount rate					
t	*1%*	*2%*	*3%*	*4%*	*5%*	*6%*	*7%*	*8%*	*9%*	*10%*
1	0.99	0.98	0.97	0.96	0.95	0.94	0.93	0.93	0.92	0.91
2	0.98	0.96	0.94	0.92	0.91	0.89	0.87	0.86	0.84	0.83
3	0.97	0.94	0.92	0.89	0.86	0.84	0.82	0.79	0.77	0.75
4	0.96	0.92	0.89	0.85	0.82	0.79	0.76	0.74	0.71	0.68
5	0.95	0.91	0.86	0.82	0.78	0.75	0.71	0.68	0.65	0.62
6	0.94	0.89	0.84	0.79	0.75	0.70	0.67	0.63	0.60	0.56
7	0.93	0.87	0.81	0.76	0.71	0.67	0.62	0.58	0.55	0.51
8	0.92	0.85	0.79	0.73	0.68	0.63	0.58	0.54	0.50	0.47
9	0.91	0.84	0.77	0.70	0.64	0.59	0.54	0.50	0.46	0.42
10	0.91	0.82	0.74	0.68	0.61	0.56	0.51	0.46	0.42	0.39
11	0.90	0.80	0.72	0.65	0.58	0.53	0.48	0.43	0.39	0.35
12	0.89	0.79	0.70	0.62	0.56	0.50	0.44	0.40	0.36	0.32
13	0.88	0.77	0.68	0.60	0.53	0.47	0.41	0.37	0.33	0.29
14	0.87	0.76	0.66	0.58	0.51	0.44	0.39	0.34	0.30	0.26
15	0.86	0.74	0.64	0.56	0.48	0.42	0.36	0.32	0.27	0.24
16	0.85	0.73	0.62	0.53	0.46	0.39	0.34	0.29	0.25	0.22
17	0.84	0.71	0.61	0.51	0.44	0.37	0.32	0.27	0.23	0.20
18	0.84	0.70	0.59	0.49	0.42	0.35	0.30	0.25	0.21	0.18
19	0.83	0.69	0.57	0.47	0.40	0.33	0.28	0.23	0.19	0.16
20	0.82	0.67	0.55	0.46	0.38	0.31	0.26	0.21	0.18	0.15

Table C Present value table: for finding the present value of recurring future cashflow

t	1%	2%	3%	4%	5%	6%	7%	8%	9%	10%
					Discount rate					
1	0.99	0.98	0.97	0.96	0.95	0.94	0.93	0.93	0.92	0.91
2	1.97	1.94	1.91	1.89	1.86	1.83	1.81	1.78	1.76	1.74
3	2.94	2.88	2.83	2.78	2.72	2.67	2.62	2.58	2.53	2.49
4	3.90	3.81	3.72	3.63	3.55	3.47	3.39	3.31	3.24	3.17
5	4.85	4.71	4.58	4.45	4.33	4.21	4.10	3.99	3.89	3.79
6	5.80	5.60	5.42	5.24	5.08	4.92	4.77	4.62	4.49	4.36
7	6.73	6.47	6.23	6.00	5.79	5.58	5.39	5.21	5.03	4.87
8	7.65	7.33	7.02	6.73	6.46	6.21	5.97	5.75	5.53	5.33
9	8.57	8.16	7.79	7.44	7.11	6.80	6.52	6.25	6.00	5.76
10	9.47	8.98	8.53	8.11	7.72	7.36	7.02	6.71	6.42	6.14
11	10.37	9.79	9.25	8.76	8.31	7.89	7.50	7.14	6.81	6.50
12	11.26	10.58	9.95	9.39	8.86	8.38	7.94	7.54	7.16	6.81
13	12.13	11.35	10.63	9.99	9.39	8.85	8.36	7.90	7.49	7.10
14	13.00	12.11	11.30	10.56	9.90	9.29	8.75	8.24	7.79	7.37
15	13.87	12.85	11.94	11.12	10.38	9.71	9.11	8.56	8.06	7.61
16	14.72	13.58	12.56	11.65	10.84	10.11	9.45	8.85	8.31	7.82
17	15.56	14.29	13.17	12.17	11.27	10.48	9.76	9.12	8.54	8.02
18	16.40	14.99	13.75	12.66	11.69	10.83	10.66	9.37	8.76	8.20
19	17.23	15.68	14.32	13.13	12.09	11.16	10.34	9.60	8.95	8.36
20	18.05	16.35	14.88	13.59	12.46	11.47	10.59	9.82	9.13	8.51

Duffy, F. (1997) *The New Office*. Conran Octopus.

Duffy, F. Laing, A. and Crisp, V. (1993) *The Responsible Workplace*. Butterworth Architecture.

Mills, E. (1994) *Building Maintenance and Preservation; Aguide to Design and Management*, 2nd. edn. Butterworth Heinemann.

Preiser, W. F. E., Rabinowitz, H. Z. and White, E. T. (1998) *Post Occupancy Evaluation*. New York Van Nostrand Reinhold.

Spedding, A, (ed.) (1994) *CIOB Handbook of Facilities Management*. Longman Scientific and Technical.

Chapter 5

Morton, R. (1996) *Design and the Economics of Building*. Spon.

Myers, D. (1995) *Economics and Property*. Spon.

Smith, M. (1996) *Interiors Management*. Upword.

Duffy, F. (1997) *The New Office*. Conran Octopus.
Duffy, F. Laing, A. and Crisp, V. (1993) *The Responsible Workplace*. Butterworth Architecture.
Mills, E. (1994) *Building Maintenance and Preservation; Aguide to Design and Management*, 2nd. edn. Butterworth Heinemann.
Preiser, W. F. E., Rabinowitz, H. Z. and White, E. T. (1998) *Post Occupancy Evaluation*. New York Van Nostrand Reinhold.
Spedding, A, (ed.) (1994) *CIOB Handbook of Facilities Management*. Longman Scientific and Technical.

Chapter 5

Morton, R. (1996) *Design and the Economics of Building*. Spon.
Myers, D. (1995) *Economics and Property*. Spon.
Smith, M. (1996) *Interiors Management*. Upword.

Table C Present value table: for finding the present value of recurring future cashflow

					Discount rate					
t	*1%*	*2%*	*3%*	*4%*	*5%*	*6%*	*7%*	*8%*	*9%*	*10%*
1	0.99	0.98	0.97	0.96	0.95	0.94	0.93	0.93	0.92	0.91
2	1.97	1.94	1.91	1.89	1.86	1.83	1.81	1.78	1.76	1.74
3	2.94	2.88	2.83	2.78	2.72	2.67	2.62	2.58	2.53	2.49
4	3.90	3.81	3.72	3.63	3.55	3.47	3.39	3.31	3.24	3.17
5	4.85	4.71	4.58	4.45	4.33	4.21	4.10	3.99	3.89	3.79
6	5.80	5.60	5.42	5.24	5.08	4.92	4.77	4.62	4.49	4.36
7	6.73	6.47	6.23	6.00	5.79	5.58	5.39	5.21	5.03	4.87
8	7.65	7.33	7.02	6.73	6.46	6.21	5.97	5.75	5.53	5.33
9	8.57	8.16	7.79	7.44	7.11	6.80	6.52	6.25	6.00	5.76
10	9.47	8.98	8.53	8.11	7.72	7.36	7.02	6.71	6.42	6.14
11	10.37	9.79	9.25	8.76	8.31	7.89	7.50	7.14	6.81	6.50
12	11.26	10.58	9.95	9.39	8.86	8.38	7.94	7.54	7.16	6.81
13	12.13	11.35	10.63	9.99	9.39	8.85	8.36	7.90	7.49	7.10
14	13.00	12.11	11.30	10.56	9.90	9.29	8.75	8.24	7.79	7.37
15	13.87	12.85	11.94	11.12	10.38	9.71	9.11	8.56	8.06	7.61
16	14.72	13.58	12.56	11.65	10.84	10.11	9.45	8.85	8.31	7.82
17	15.56	14.29	13.17	12.17	11.27	10.48	9.76	9.12	8.54	8.02
18	16.40	14.99	13.75	12.66	11.69	10.83	10.66	9.37	8.76	8.20
19	17.23	15.68	14.32	13.13	12.09	11.16	10.34	9.60	8.95	8.36
20	18.05	16.35	14.88	13.59	12.46	11.47	10.59	9.82	9.13	8.51

Table C Present value table: for finding the present value of recurring future cashflow

					Discount rate					
t	1%	2%	3%	4%	5%	6%	7%	8%	9%	10%
1	0.99	0.98	0.97	0.96	0.95	0.94	0.93	0.93	0.92	0.91
2	1.97	1.94	1.91	1.89	1.86	1.83	1.81	1.78	1.76	1.74
3	2.94	2.88	2.83	2.78	2.72	2.67	2.62	2.58	2.53	2.49
4	3.90	3.81	3.72	3.63	3.55	3.47	3.39	3.31	3.24	3.17
5	4.85	4.71	4.58	4.45	4.33	4.21	4.10	3.99	3.89	3.79
6	5.80	5.60	5.42	5.24	5.08	4.92	4.77	4.62	4.49	4.36
7	6.73	6.47	6.23	6.00	5.79	5.58	5.39	5.21	5.03	4.87
8	7.65	7.33	7.02	6.73	6.46	6.21	5.97	5.75	5.53	5.33
9	8.57	8.16	7.79	7.44	7.11	6.80	6.52	6.25	6.00	5.76
10	9.47	8.98	8.53	8.11	7.72	7.36	7.02	6.71	6.42	6.14
11	10.37	9.79	9.25	8.76	8.31	7.89	7.50	7.14	6.81	6.50
12	11.26	10.58	9.95	9.39	8.86	8.38	7.94	7.54	7.16	6.81
13	12.13	11.35	10.63	9.99	9.39	8.85	8.36	7.90	7.49	7.10
14	13.00	12.11	11.30	10.56	9.90	9.29	8.75	8.24	7.79	7.37
15	13.87	12.85	11.94	11.12	10.38	9.71	9.11	8.56	8.06	7.61
16	14.72	13.58	12.56	11.65	10.84	10.11	9.45	8.85	8.31	7.82
17	15.56	14.29	13.17	12.17	11.27	10.48	9.76	9.12	8.54	8.02
18	16.40	14.99	13.75	12.66	11.69	10.83	10.66	9.37	8.76	8.20
19	17.23	15.68	14.32	13.13	12.09	11.16	10.34	9.60	8.95	8.36
20	18.05	16.35	14.88	13.59	12.46	11.47	10.59	9.82	9.13	8.51

Table D Sinking fund factors

			Interest earned			
t	*3%*	*4%*	*5%*	*6%*	*7%*	*8%*
1	1.00000	1.00000	1.00000	1.00000	1.00000	1.00000
2	0.49261	0.49019	0.48780	0.48543	0.48309	0.48076
3	0.32353	0.32034	0.31720	0.31410	0.31105	0.30803
4	0.23902	0.23549	0.23201	0.22859	0.22522	0.22192
5	0.18835	0.18462	0.18097	0.17739	0.17389	0.17045
6	0.15459	0.15076	0.14701	0.14336	0.13979	0.13631
7	0.13050	0.12660	0.12281	0.11913	0.11555	0.11207
8	0.11245	0.10852	0.10472	0.10103	0.09746	0.09401
9	0.09843	0.09449	0.09069	0.08702	0.08348	0.08007
10	0.08723	0.08329	0.07950	0.07586	0.07237	0.06902
11	0.07807	0.07414	0.07038	0.06679	0.06335	0.06007
12	0.07046	0.06655	0.06282	0.05927	0.05590	0.05269
13	0.06402	0.06014	0.05645	0.05296	0.04965	0.04652
14	0.05852	0.05466	0.05102	0.04758	0.04434	0.04129
15	0.05376	0.04994	0.04634	0.04296	0.03979	0.03682
16	0.04961	0.04582	0.04226	0.03895	0.03585	0.03297
17	0.04595	0.04219	0.03869	0.03544	0.03242	0.02962
18	0.04270	0.03899	0.03554	0.03235	0.02941	0.02670
19	0.03981	0.03613	0.03274	0.02962	0.02675	0.02412
20	0.03721	0.03358	0.03024	0.02718	0.02439	0.02185

Appendix 2

Useful Reading

Chapter 1

Burberry, P. (1997) *Environment and Services* Longman Scientific.

Chadderton, D. (1995) *Building Services Engineering* E & FN Spon.

CIBSE (1986) *CIBSE Guide*, 5 vols. Chartered Institute of Building Services Engineers.

Curd, E and Howard, C. (1996) *Introduction to Building Services.* MacMillan.

Greeno, R. (1997) *Building Services Technology & Design.* Addison Wesley Longman.

Hall, F. (1994) *Building Services & Equipment*, vols 1 and 2. Longman Scientific.

Stollard, P. and Abrahams, J. (1995) *Fire from First Principles.* E & FN Spon.

Chapter 2

Card, R. (1994) *Law for Estate Management Students.* Butterworths.

Keenan, D. (1994) *English Law.* Cavendish.

Galbraith, A. (1993) *Building and Land Management Law for Students.* Newnes.

Holyoak, J. (1992) *Negligence in Building Law.* Blackwell.

Chapter 3

The Energy Efficiency Office (see Appendix 3 for address) produces a wide range of leaflets available either free or at a very small cost. There are several hundred available, and many are specific to given building types, eg hotels, retail, offices.

Steel, M. and Heath, R. (1998) *Energy Efficient Building Use.* Chandos.

Moss, K. (1997) *Energy Management and Operating Costs.* Spon.

Chapter 4

Brand, S. (1997) *How Buildings Learn: What happens after they're Built*, 2nd edn. Phoenix Illustrated.

Chanter, B. and Swallow, P. (1996) *Building Maintenance Management.* Blackwell Science.

Duffy, F. (1997) *The New Office*. Conran Octopus.

Duffy, F. Laing, A. and Crisp, V. (1993) *The Responsible Workplace*. Butterworth Architecture.

Mills, E. (1994) *Building Maintenance and Preservation; Aguide to Design and Management*, 2nd. edn. Butterworth Heinemann.

Preiser, W. F. E., Rabinowitz, H. Z. and White, E. T. (1998) *Post Occupancy Evaluation*. New York Van Nostrand Reinhold.

Spedding, A, (ed.) (1994) *CIOB Handbook of Facilities Management*. Longman Scientific and Technical.

Chapter 5

Morton, R. (1996) *Design and the Economics of Building*. Spon.

Myers, D. (1995) *Economics and Property*. Spon.

Smith, M. (1996) *Interiors Management*. Upword.

Appendix 3

Useful Addresses

The Energy Office
ETSU
Hartwell
Oxfordshire
OX11 0RA

Local Energy Efficiency Centres:

Scotland
New St Andrews House
EDINBURGH
Scotland EH1 3TA
Tel: 0131 244 1200
Fax: 0131 244 4860

East Midlands
Cranbrook House
Cranbrook Street
NOTTINGHAM
NG1 1EY
Tel: 0115 935 2292
Fax: 0115 935 2293

South West
Government Office South West
Tollgate House
Houlton Street
BRISTOL BS2 9DJ
Tel: 0117 987 8665
Fax: 0119 987 8269

Yorkshire & Humberside
City House
New Station Street
LEEDS LS1 4JD
Tel: 0113 283 6376
Fax: 0113 283 6375

Wales
Industry & Trading Department
Cathays Park
CARDIFF CF1 1NQ
Tel: 01222 823126
Fax: 01222 640458

South East
Charles House
Room 551
375 Kensington High Street
LONDON W14 8QH
Tel: 020 7605 9160
Fax: 020 7605 9170

North East
Wellbar House
Gallowgate
NEWCASTLE UPON TYNE
NE1 4TD
Tel: 0191 201 3343
Fax: 0191 230 2049

West Midlands
Five Ways Tower
Frederick Road
BIRMINGHAM B15 1SJ
Tel: 0121 626 222
Fax: 0121 626 3219

Northern Ireland
Department of Economic
Development
Netherleigh House
Massey Avenue
BELFAST
Northern Ireland BT4 2JT
Tel: 0232 529 900
Fax: 0232 629 550

North West
Sunley Tower
Piccadilly Plaza
MANCHESTER M1 4BA
Tel: 0161 952 4282
Fax: 0161 838 5467

Eastern
Heron House
49–53 Goldington Road
BEDFORD MK40 3LL
Tel: 01234 276194
Fax: 01234 276313

The Chartered Institute of Building Services Engineers
222 Balham High Road
LONDON
SW12 9BS

The Royal Institute of Chartered Surveyors
12 Great George Street
LONDON
SW1 4AP

The Royal Institute of British Architects
66 Portland Place
LONDON
W1N 4AD

The British Institute of Facilities Management
67 High Street
SAFFRON WALDEN
Essex
CB10 1AA

Glossary

Absorption cycle system. A more environmentally friendly air-conditioning system in which the vapour from the coolant is absorbed by a process which prevents its release into the atmosphere.

Active fire protection. This involves the use of mechanical devices which are activated in response to the outbreak of fire. The devices may be installed individually or as part of a fire detection system or firefighting installation.

Active security measures. Security installations that involve the use of mechanical and other devices to detect unauthorised building users and to warn of their presence.

Active systems. Anything in a building that consumes energy itself, such as lights.

Air change rate. The number of times per hour that it is necessary to renew the air in each room or area of a building in order to maintain a healthy level of breathable air and to avoid any over-concentration of carbon dioxide. Typical air change rates per hour for particular room uses are 4–6 for offices, 6–10 for conference rooms and 10–15 for restaurants.

Air-water system. An air-conditioning system in which air and chilled or heated water are used to maintain comfortable working conditions.

All-air system. An air-conditioning system in which only air is used to control the internal environment.

Analogue. This type of component makes use of hands or a pointer to indicate information and can be based on either a clockwork mechanism or microchip technology.

Asset register. A list of properties owned by an organisation, detailing their main attributes.

Ballast. The control gear in a light fitting.

Bank of lifts. A term used to describe a group of two or more lifts.

Baseline alternative. This is the decision not to go ahead with a project, which all other possibilities are compared to. For instance the costs and savings of double glazing are compared to those of single glazing, which is the baseline.

Base year. The first year of a study period where t = 0.

Building Regulations (strictly speaking The Building Regulations). The mandatory minimum construction standards for building works and services in new and existing buildings. The standards are under constant review and revision to higher levels of application.

Chilled beam. An air cooling system that makes use of cooled water circulated via finned tubes in beams or small pipes in ceiling tiles (where it is known as a chilled ceiling system). Ventilation is provided separately by either a **variable air volume (VAV)** air-conditioning system or by a more simple mechanical ventilation system or even by openable windows.

Cold bridge. This occurs where the insulating envelope of a building is bridged between the external and internal faces allowing the transmission of colder temperatures to the inside face. It often leads to condensation problems and can occur in both framed and masonry construction.

Combined heat and power unit (CHP). Installing a single unit that provides power for a building and uses the heat generated as a by-product to heat the building. Such units can be expensive to install and will only be cost effective if both heat and power are needed for over 4,500 hours per year.

Compact fluorescent lamp (CFL). A fluorescent bulb, normally with integral control gear, that fits into a conventional light fitting. It uses about 25 per cent of the energy of a tungsten filament bulb (the type normally used) but produces a slightly less bright light.

Compartment. An area of a building that is completely enclosed by fire and smoke resistant walls, floors and ceilings to prevent the spread of fire from adjoining compartments and to aid the **means of escape.**

Complementary systems. Systems which improve the performance of other systems, such as a computer to control heating and lighting in a 'smart' building.

Condensing boiler. An extremely efficient type of boiler which extracts more of the heat from the flue gases via an enlarged or secondary heat exchanger. It is environmentally friendly as less CO_2 and other obnoxious emissions are produced.

Consumer control unit. The building user's distribution board for the electrical system in a small to medium-sized building. It contains a master switch and controls for all circuits within the building.

Cost-effective. A cost-effective component or system is the one that maximises **net savings** or minimises **life cycle costs.**

Cost of capital. See **discount rate.**

Curtilage. The total area of a building and the land surrounding it.

Digital. This type of component makes use of digits to display information and is based on microchip technology.

Direct policy. Government regulatory policy, such as anti-pollution laws.

Discount rate. The percentage used to convert future cashflows into present value terms, based on interest rates and inflation. It is expressed as a decimal function, so 8 per cent appears as 0.08. It is sometimes known as 'cost of capital'.

Discretionary system. One that is not necessary but may be cost-effective, for instance double glazing.

Distribution board. The building user's control unit for all the electrical circuits supplying power, light and heat within a larger building. It contains master switches, switchgear and fuses and may well control sub-distribution boards.

Draw-off point. A tap, valve or other component from which water can be drawn.

Dry riser. A vertical water pipe that is kept empty until required for firefighting purposes. It is installed in an unheated building or one where there is insufficient water pressure at the highest floor levels. The maximum height of a dry main is 60 metres above which a wet riser must be installed. The base of the dry riser is left accessible to the fire service so that it can be connected to a fire tender or the nearest fire hydrant.

Dry system. A water system that is kept dry until needed, usually when there is a fire. Systems in unheated areas or where there is a great likelihood of significant damage to a building's contents from leakage, eg in a warehouse, are commonly maintained in a dry state.

Earth bund (or **berm** in USA). A built-up embankment of spoil and topsoil placed against an external wall to provide weather protection.

Ecolabel. A certificate showing that a product has a low environmental impact.

Effectiveness. Achieving the best balance between **efficiency** and quality, while taking into account the different priorities of relevant groups and individuals.

Efficiency. Relates to maximising quantity while minimising cost and delivering on time.

Embodied energy. A complex procedure by which components are graded for the 'green' credentials by measuring how much energy goes into producing them. Bricks, for instance, consume energy in the quarrying of the clay, in the firing process in the kiln and in their transportation to site.

Energy audit. A survey of a building, or group of buildings, and its/their management to judge the **effectiveness** of the measures to save energy.

Facilities management. The coordination between work, the workplace and people within a broader practice environment.

Fire engineering. Also called fire safety engineering. This is a flexible design approach in which all design elements of a building are reviewed holistically to arrive at an optimum solution for fire safety.

Fiscal policy. Anything related to government taxation or spending.

Heat exchanger. A coiled pipe containing hot water that transfers heat as it passes through the water stored in the cylinder.

Heat gain. Heat emitted from occupants, lights and other fittings, computers, machinery and plant that contributes to the internal temperature of a building.

Heat pump. A device which, working in much the same way as a refrigerator, absorbs heat from a low-temperature source and through the use of a condenser gives out heat at a higher temperature.

Heat recovery system. A system attached to the exhaust or air extract of a mechanical ventilation or air-conditioning system which enables a relatively high percentage (65–85 per cent) of the latent (or unused) heat from the outflowing air to be reused.

High-efficiency boiler. This has a more efficient heat exchanger and better casing insulation than a conventional boiler but is less efficient than a condensing boiler.

Hydraulic lift. A modern form of lift that uses oil pressure to power the process. Some older hydraulic lifts that are still in use are powered by a high-pressure water main.

Impeller. A multi-bladed drum-shaped fan unit.

Landfill tax. Introduced in 1996 to discourage landfill dumping. It is a tax on the volume of material dumped. The intention is to make it cost-effective for companies to recycle or burn waste instead.

Leading question. One which prompts a specific answer, such as 'Did you see a man wearing a balaclava and brandishing a gun?'

Life cycle cost method. The 'cradle to grave' costs of a project from inception through to (and including) disposal or scrapping when a system becomes obsolete.

Luminaire. Another term for a light fitting.

Mandatory system. See **baseline alternative**.

Miniature circuit breaker (MCB). A modern completely sealed circuit control unit controlled by a simple switch. An MCB cannot be overridden once a fault develops in the circuit until the fault has been repaired.

Minimum acceptable rate of return. The minimum percentage return a company will accept on an investment. It is the same as the **discount rate** in most companies.

Net savings method. A development of the **life cycle costs** method which expresses the cash a system saves above its life cycle costs.

Obsolescence. The process of diminishing fitness for purpose.

Off-peak. A cheaper night-time tariff for the supply of electricity that is used particularly for night storage heating systems.

On-peak. The standard tariff for the supply of electricity.

Opportunity cost. The money forgone by using capital for one project rather than another. If £10,000 was taken from a savings account and invested in cavity wall insulation the opportunity cost would be the interest lost. At 8 per cent this would be £800 per year.

Option appraisal. The systematic analysis of the relative advantages and disadvantages of alternative options, with regard to specific objectives, and taking into account both monetary and non-monetary aspects.

Packaged plant. A complete prefabricated air-conditioning system of limited capacity that can be easily installed to service one zone or space. Capital cost is low and running costs are average.

Passive fire protection. This is an approach to fire prevention and control that makes use of appropriate design and selection of construction materials rather than mechanical devices to prevent fire and its spread.

Passive security measures. These involve integrating into the design of the fabric of a building or security area non-mechanical means of restricting or controlling entry.

Passive stack ventilation (PSV). This involves the use of one or more vertical stacks or ducts in a naturally ventilated building. The effect of pressure differential and wind across the top of the stack results in increased air movement. It can also be used to reduce the risk of condensation.

Passive systems. Building components that do not use energy themselves after installation, such as walls.

Payback. The period of time it takes for an investment to break even.

Place of safety. An area where the occupants of a building are in no danger from a fire.

Plenum system. A mechanical ventilation or air-conditioning system in which the pressure of the air in the building is above atmospheric pressure.

Point of use water heater. Smaller gas or electric instantaneous water heaters which are positioned next to sinks or hand-basins. Each heats cold mains-fed water as it passes through the appliance.

Post-occupancy evaluation. The process of evaluating a building after it has been occupied, in order to determine whether or not it fulfils the original brief or the needs of the current users.

Precycling. Cutting down on waste by minimising the amount of material used in the production process.

Present value terms. Future cash flows expressed at their current value.

Primary circuit. The flow and return pipes in a heating system which circulate hot water between the boiler and the cylinder.

Private Finance Initiative and **Public–Private Partnerships**. Government schemes to encourage the formation of partnerships between public sector organisations and private companies in order to build and/or manage a property or group of properties.

Radial circuit. These are installed in larger buildings and those with a higher electrical demand. They radiate out from the **distribution board** rather than loop around a building as with a **ring main**.

Radial duct system. A warm air heating system with longer ducts serving louvre-controlled wall or floor grilles positioned around the perimeter of a building.

Real price. The price of something once inflation has been taken into account. If electricity is expected to increase in price by 5 per cent over the next year and inflation is 3 per cent the real price increase is 2 per cent.

Retrofit. Adding new systems or components to an existing building.

Revocation. The withdrawal of an offer in negotiating a contract.

Right of audience. The right to be heard in court.

Ring main. Also known as a ring circuit or final circuit. This is the individually wired circuit that runs in a completely closed loop from the **consumer control unit** to the various outlets There are always separate ring mains for each type of use, eg lighting, power or heating.

Schedule of rates. A list of unit prices for specific items of work (the rates may be agreed by negotiation or competitive tender).

Semi-exposed space. An area within a building which is not fully enclosed and is therefore subject to the effect of external temperatures (eg a garage or a loading bay).

Sensitivity analysis. A method by which some variables in a calculation are altered to see how risky a project is in the event of unforeseen changes in circumstances.

Sick building syndrome. A range of illnesses that may be suffered individually or in any combination and affect the occupants of a building to differing degrees. Symptoms include headaches, irritations of the eye, nose and throat, mental fatigue, physical lethargy and dizziness. The illness is more commonly associated with hermetically sealed buildings and air-conditioning systems than with those buildings making use of simpler mechanical or natural ventilation systems. Poor maintenance levels are thought to be a contributory factor. Suspected causes range from dust, mites and micro-organisms to high air temperatures, poor humidity levels, poor lighting and even the glues used in building materials.

Sinking fund. A cash sum set aside each year in an interest-earning account to provide a lump sum for future expenditure. Tax allowances are available on some sinking funds.

Smart building. A building with computer controlled environmental systems.

Smart glass. Also known as intelligent glass, it is capable of varying its optical and thermal transmittance properties.

Solar gain. Heat gained from exposure to the sun.

Solar shading. The provision of deeply overhanging eaves or external shading devices above windows to provide protection from solar gain and glare.

Standard assessment procedure. SAP is a standardised method by which a building's energy efficiency is calculated by specialists.

Stub duct system. A warm air heating system in which short horizontal or vertical ducts are installed around a centrally positioned boiler or heating unit.

Study period. The period of time over which a project is analysed.

Thermostatic radiator valve (TRV). A temperature thermostat fitted to an individual radiator instead of an ordinary 'open or closed' valve which is linked to a room thermostat. The TRV enables the temperature of each room or zone to be specifically regulated.

Trickle ventilator. A small, easily controlled ventilator normally installed in a window or its frame to allow background ventilation without the necessity of opening the window.

U-value. The thermal efficiency of any part of a building such as the wall or roof. The lower the better.

Variable air volume (VAV). A type of **all-air** air conditioning system which can be zoned to service individual rooms or areas. The delivered air must be all heated or all cooled throughout the building, although some local control is possible.

Vapour check. Also known as a vapour barrier or vapour control layer. It is a sheet of vapour resistant material placed on the internal face of any thermal insulation in a roof, wall or floor. This prevents warm moist air within the building coming into contact with the colder part of the structure and condensing.

Wet riser. A vertical pipe that is permanently filled with water in case of fire. It can serve any height of building but usually requires a pump to be installed to maintain the water pressure when in use. There should also be a suction tank provided to avoid direct pumping from the water main.

Wet system. A water system that is kept fully charged with water at all times.